Gone Huntin'

A Generation of Hunting in Northern British Columbia

by
Pat Ferguson

Fergie's Follies
P.O. Box 475
Clearwater, B.C. Canada V0E 1N0

National Library of Canada Cataloguing in Publication Data

Ferguson, Pat, 1948-
  Gone huntin' : a generation of hunting in northern British Columbia / by Pat Ferguson.

  ISBN 0-9731877-0-0 (bound). — ISBN 0-9731877-1-9 (pbk.)

  1. Ferguson, Pat, 1948- 2. Big game hunting—British Columbia, Northern. 3. Hunters—British Columbia, Northern—Biography. I. Title.

SK17.F47A3 2002   799.2'6'092   C2002-911253-2

Published by:
  Fergie's Follies
  P.O. Box 475
  Clearwater, B.C. Canada V0E 1N0

All photographs by the author unless otherwise credited. All illustrations are protected by copyright and may not be reproduced in any form without prior written consent of the publisher.

Cover Photo: Pat Ferguson and son Chuck with 9 ½ inch and 11 ⅜ inch billy goats.

Designed by: Murphy Shewchuk, Sonotek® Publishing Ltd.

Printed in Canada by: Friesens Corp., Altona, Manitoba.

Pat Ferguson

Table of Contents

Dedication 5

Acknowledgments 5

Introduction. 6

My Favourite Hunting Partner... 7

1   The First Time is the Best.... 8

2   Ida Tours Club Moose.... 16

3   Solo for Stones: The First Sheep Hunt... 25

4   Dodd's First Moose... 52

5   Moose and Caribou Hunt With the Good Ol' Boys... . 59

6   Ida Bags a Pachyderm.... 74

7   The Family that Hunts Together, Grunts Together... . 81

8   Glacier Billy... 89

9   Spatsizi Caribou.... 93

10   Stones in a Rock Pile.... 109

11   Gettin' Walter's Goat.... 125

12   "Incoming Moose!". 130

13   Caribou in Paradise... 136

14   High Tension Grizzlies.... 157

15   The Fizz Bang Moose... 176

About the Author. 192

Dedication

To four youngsters who left us far too soon...
Leland Myles Bradford
Scott Murray Jackson
Daphne Constance Ferguson
Charles Michael Ferguson

Acknowledgments

The original idea for this book came from the many people who have watched my slide shows over the years. Some of them were hunters, but most were not. In any event, I would like to thank them for planting the seed.

I wrote the entire manuscript with pencil and paper. After completing each chapter, I placed it in a folder and handed it to my mule deer-hunting partner, Bill Ludtke. He, in turn, provided me with invaluable constructive criticism and a few good general pointers. Howie Baker did the primary edit and assisted me with more helpful advice. My good friend Dave Garner, a connoisseur of disgusting humour and single malt Scotch, spent countless hours at the computer cussing in seventeen languages as we slowly brought the manuscript together.

Many of my twenty-year-old photographs would have been useless were it not for the efforts of Ryan Lepp at Private Eye Imaging. A monumental thanks to Wendy Liddle who, with her cartoon art, helped to make me look nearly as nuts as I really am.

Tackling this project was made less terrifying with guidance from the book *How to Self-Publish and Make Money* by Marion Crook and Nancy Wise. Murphy Shewchuk, at Sonotek® Publishing Ltd., worked his magic to pour everything together for the final product, of which I am extremely proud.

Finally, I would like to thank all of the talented Bush Pilots for bringing us back alive.

•••

Introduction

Although this book is primarily about hunting, I have concentrated not on the taking of animal lives nor the size of the animals taken, but on the adventure of the hunt. I will not endeavor to explain why I hunt nor to apologize for being a hunter. I feel that there is no need since my eyes face forward like every other predator on earth.

Out of respect for my fellow resident hunters, our many species of wildlife and the guide/outfitters who nurture and manage them, I have left out specific names of particular lakes and rivers. I have discovered, over the years, that if your peers deem you worthy, they will share their special places with you.

I have made it my mission to take my children to the mountains and teach them the ways of our precious wildlife. With good scientific game management and a lot less politics, my grandchildren will have the opportunity to hunt these same mountains.

A wise man once said, "Hunt with your children today and you won't hunt for them tomorrow."

Pat Ferguson

•••

My Favourite Hunting Partner...

If, in their lifetime, a person has one or two good friends, they can count themselves fortunate.

If, on the other hand, they have one or more good hunting partners, they are, indeed, among the very fortunate.

I learned, early on in my hunting career, that an unworthy hunting partner is far worse than no partner at all. As a consequence, I developed a habit of quietly studying any prospective partners before committing myself to any major adventures with them.

Ida Lucette Ferguson

Many years later, I am proud to say that I have shared the mountains with several very worthy hunting partners. We have endured rain, wind, driving snow, and enjoyed beautiful sunny days as we back-packed for days on end through the mountains in our search for Sheep, Goat, or Caribou. Some times we returned with game on our pack frames, and many times we didn't. It really didn't matter one way or the other, as each trip was an adventure like no other.

You will read about some very special hunting partners in the following chapters, but I must proudly state that my favourite hunting partner of all is:

My lovely wife, Ida,
who shoots 'em
guts 'em
and skins 'em!!!

Just the greatest partner I could have ever hoped for!!

•••

7

1
The First Time is the Best...

As the de Havilland Beaver roared to life, the entire world seemed to cower and shake. With the chill breeze, he was on the step and airborne within seconds. A few seconds more and he was throttled back and diving over the edge of the plateau.

The sudden silence was deafening, welling up like distant thunder. We stood there in silence, not moving or speaking. Finally — real solitude. Then, a quiet rustling of wings, tiny bird voices and within minutes, a total riot of bird song erupted from the blazing red arctic birch, yellow wolf willow, and stunted alpine balsam.

I turned to Ida and said, "Well, what do you think?"

With an apprehensive look at me and another glance around, she said, "Well, it sure as hell is wild up here!"

This was my very first fly-in hunt, and I wanted to share it with my lovely wife, who, I might add, seemed fearful I was only trying to get rid of her. For weeks before the hunt, she would wake up at night in the midst of a grizzly bear attack. I would wake her and say "Honey it's only me!" This would really send her into orbit, since I'm the wise guy who came up with the idea.

We spent weeks getting our gear ready, double-checking everything, trying to imagine every scenario that might befall us. Finally, although we didn't have the best of gear in those days, I felt we could survive a week or two in the wilds.

After dropping our three children off with the Claridges in Stewart, we embarked on the five-hour drive to Dease Lake. Finally, after an eventful trip of choking dust and bottomless potholes, we spent the night with our friends, Myles and Sherry Bradford, two of the best guide/outfitters in the business.

Ida visited with Sherry while I walked over to the BC-Yukon float base to make sure that all was still a go for our morning flight. The weather was holding. There was a big high-pressure system over northern BC that would bring warm sunny days and clear cold nights. It doesn't get any better than this for hunting caribou and hanging meat.

That night, Myles radioed home from one of his camps. As tired and worn out as he was, he hopped into his Cub and flew home for a visit.

Over a cold beer, I told Myles about Ida's fear of grizzlies, and he assured me that everything would be just fine. He said that these were not the spoiled park bears, they were the hunted bears, and so steer clear of man every chance they get. As the years went by, I lost my fear of grizzlies but I gained greater respect, the more I learned about them.

Our flight was scheduled for mid-morning, so I took my time unloading and checking my gear at the float base. My excitement level went through the roof when the Beaver came in with a pair of tired, (a little ripe) and happy hunters. The reasons for their happiness were tangled around the neck, and poking in the ribs and backside of the guy in the back.

After pulling three or four hundred pounds of caribou meat out of the side door of the Beaver, it was time to rescue the back seat pilot from what had been his cozy nest for the past hour. With much twisting, pulling, and muffled cussing the pilot extracted two beautiful sets of caribou antlers and passed them to their proud owners. It took me about two seconds to wrestle the prizes away from these guys, so that I could have a good look at them. One thing that struck me was the unique smell of the meat. I could only imagine how good it was going to be on the table.

It was our turn to load up when refueling was complete. The pilot couldn't believe how little gear we carried. Even with the inflatable boat, there was plenty of room left inside the aircraft. Ida climbed in to her seat by the side door and I sat in the front passenger seat. As the pilot untied the plane, and pushed away from the float I thought, "By God, we're really going to make it happen!" Safely away from the dock the pilot climbed in and closed the door.

He's all business now, as he flips a few switches, moves a few controls and flashes her up. As we taxi down the lake, he puts on his seat belt, then grabs a hastily made sandwich out of his shirt, and takes a big bite out of it. He goes over his checklist of switches and gauges: all is ready. He pulls out a map and double checks our destination, folds the map, and stows it in the door pocket. Next, he puts on his headset, and adjusts the radio. He has a good look around for other aircraft and begins his take-off run. In a few noisy seconds, we are in the air and pointed in the right direction.

Iwas grinning from ear to ear, as I looked back to see if Ida was still with us. The look on her face was not unlike that of a cat about to go under the water with a brick tied to its tail. I quickly looked forward again, trying to pretend I didn't notice. Fortunately, the flight was uneventful, and after a while, I think I detected a trace of a smile from the back seat.

As our lake came into view, the excitement was overpowering. Such a wild and beautiful piece of country — and it would be home for the next ten days. As is usual with BC-Yukon pilots, the landing was flawless and the pilot spoke for the first time since take-off nearly an hour before. We both watched for hidden rocks as we drifted quietly up to the beach. We quickly unloaded our gear and gave him a shove back out to deeper water. With several more flights to make, he had no time to visit.

Fig 1:
"We found the perfect spot with a little creek running through it."

We decided after a quick look around to try and find a more protected area to set up camp. Down the beach about half a mile we found the perfect spot with a little creek running through it, and a fringe of willows on the lakeside to break the wind. We inflated the raft, and putting our gear aboard we headed for our new site. A constant breeze kept the bugs away, making setting up camp almost fun.

By the time camp was set up and lunch out of the way, it was mid-afternoon and time for a look at the country. A low grassy ridge above camp provided a commanding view of the far side of the lake and most of the near side as well. Within two minutes we had spotted four caribou bulls feeding on a meadow directly across the lake. One was a medium sized bull with long back tines that looked like they crossed. Two looked like twins, with long, wide, heavy beams. The fourth was a tremendous big bull. Unlike the other bulls, which were still in velvet, this guy had ragged velvet hanging all torn and tattered from a huge set of bloody antlers. It was hard to get a good look at his bez and shovel set-up because of all the velvet hanging down. But it was easy to see the tops. He had massive palmation, and lots of heavy long points. It was getting late in the day, so we spent the remaining daylight watching the bulls feeding and resting, under a typically spectacular northern sunset.

Somewhere around daylight, I rolled out of the sack and discovered to my amazement, that Ida had not been eaten alive by a grizzly after all. I promptly woke her and broke the good news to her, as I struggled into my frozen boots.

Out on the lake, a loon yodelled in the thick morning fog. Heavy frost had frozen our water pail solid and transformed the whole country into a wonderland. As our coffee perked and Ida got dressed, I took a short stroll on the beach to work out a few kinks, and drink in the fresh mountain air. My nostrils tingled at all the smells of autumn.

We stood side by side on the shore and enjoyed our morning coffee. Suddenly, I spotted something out in the fog swimming toward us. Through my bino's it looked like an Otter, but I couldn't get them focused properly. When I took my bino's down I realized the fog was playing tricks on me. It was not an otter forty yards away, but a lemming, forty feet away. As he neared shore, I stepped in front of him and put my hand just under the water. He swam right into my hand and I lifted him up for a closer look. Having 'lemming-paddled' a mile across the lake he was quite content to sit in my cupped hand and rest for a few minutes. When he became restless I set him back on the beach, and he carried on — straight north.

After breakfast, we threw our gear into the raft and headed across the lake. From shore to shore, were scattered the bodies of lemmings that didn't make the cold, wet journey. They were all floating with just their little frost covered heads above water. When we reached the far shore we found dead lemmings every two feet, washed back on the South shore that they had started from only hours before. It seems that our little friend back at camp was a hardy little guy.

We pulled our raft up into the short willows and started up the side of a high butte to see if we could spot the four bulls. By the time we were high enough to see everything, the fog was burning off and the sun was producing some heat. We sat back and had a good look at some of the most beautiful real estate in Canada. We were in no rush to do anything but relax and let this hunt develop naturally. Time and weather were on our side. From our vantage point, we could see for sixty miles west to the Coast Range, and about the same to the south. Recent heavy frost had taken care of most of the black flies, so a nice quiet snooze on the tundra was in order.

About mid-day, we decided to head slowly down the mountain and try a different vantage point. We were just getting down into a few scattered patches of stunted balsam when Ida suddenly erupted into incoherent babble behind me. One look told me her eyes were indeed brown and big. Finally, the word "caribou!" came out of her, as she pointed frantically to the east. A quick squint to the east told the 'Bwana' that indeed a fine caribou bull was approaching.

He was casually following a cow along the mountainside, loading up on 'groceries'. The two were about two hundred yards away, and had not spotted us yet. We ducked into a shallow gully, then crawled out beside a scrub balsam and prepared for the shot. About the time Ida was ready, the cow spotted us and ran uphill to our left. The bull looked up at her, giving a clear neck shot, and it was all over but the hard work.

After a lengthy photo session, we got down to work, and soon had him piled up in manageable chunks. It wasn't long, however, before we discovered that I didn't have enough rope on my pack frame to tie the meat. Ida was busy removing long strips of velvet from the antlers and it struck me ... I grabbed a strip and gave it a good pull. It held together. I took all the rope off the pack frame, tied a few strips of velvet together, then added the rope to the end. Luckily, it held together until we made it to the lake. Since then, I always have at least forty feet of light rope on my pack.

By the time we got back to camp, it was late afternoon. While dinner was cooking, I looked across the lake with my bino's and saw four fine bulls in the same meadow as the day before. We hadn't spotted them from the mountain because of the long narrow meadow, and the low angle of view. We would try for one of these bulls in the morning, then get the rest of the meat from the first bull the next day.

In the morning, we waited in camp for the fog to lift, spotted the bulls, and then crossed the lake about a mile down from them.

A long, slow stalk brought us to what I thought was the right meadow. We approached it cautiously from the top end, but could spot nothing.

On the far side of the meadow was a low ridge covered in arctic birch. Not wanting to be caught in the open, we crossed the sixty yards quickly. At the very edge of the meadow, were two big beds with the grass still popping up in them. I quickly looked all around, and there, on the side we had just come from were the twins. They were about a hundred and fifty yards away, angling slowly toward us with their heads down, feeding.

I didn't want to shoot offhand, so we moved back to dry ground and sat down. While getting into position for my shot, I looked for a shooting lane through the scattered balsam. Both bulls looked the same, so when the second bull passed the gap, I squeezed off a shot. They both stopped, looked around, then kept on feeding. My little 85 grain .243 bullet had blown up on a branch. As they passed the next gap, I squeezed off another shot. That one did the trick. He didn't know what hit him and neither did his partner, who fed peacefully away, out of sight.

Waiting a few minutes to make sure there was no movement, we made our way across the meadow. What a beautiful fat bull he was. If we had stayed where we were ten minutes before, the bulls would have walked right up to us.

The afternoon sun was warming things up considerably, so we took a few photos and got down to work. The first load to the lake took only twenty minutes; this was quite a treat after the three-mile pack yesterday. By late afternoon, we had all the meat hanging in meat bags back in camp. A quick dish pan bath, and a change of clothes and we were ready for dinner.

On the menu was day-old caribou filet with corn and potatoes. Dessert was more caribou fillet, corn and potatoes. By the time I had finished eating, I looked like a poisoned pup, and felt like a contented wolf. Ida washed the dishes while I made us each a cup of tea and got our living room ready — our upside down raft on the beach, facing another glorious sunset.

Morning found us crossing the lake for the last load of meat from the first bull. I wasn't too worried about the meat, as I had left a booby trap (my underwear) hanging from a stick. By mid afternoon we were on our way back across the lake with the last load of meat. What a shame. Three days to go, and all we had to do was relax, and explore the endless miles of tundra. That night I drank tea and took it easy on our inflatable chesterfield, and coached Ida as she caught and released several fat grayling in the setting sun.

The next morning, we stayed in bed until the sun burned the frost off the tent. Coffee, followed by steak and eggs, got our day off to a good start. After breakfast, we sat on our up-turned raft and enjoyed a second cup of coffee. With our feet less than three feet from the water, we weren't surprised when a little sandpiper worked his way right up to our boots. Within a few short days, he would be in the midst of his long journey south.

Fig 2:
"The bull looked up at her, giving a clear neck shot, and it was all over..."

Later in the morning, at the east end of the lake, we discovered a sad sight. A mother sea duck was trying to nurture two fat fuzzy ducklings. They were huddled on top of a small flat rock out in the narrows, with barely a trace of flight feathers; they were destined to be fox feed with the first good skim of ice.

A short climb put us on top of a ridge with a panoramic view of the country to the east. It was from this ridge that we would plan some of our future adventures.

As the sun set that evening, I could detect the whispering chatter of a Super Cub, but couldn't spot him. Suddenly, he blasted over the ridge behind us, just above the treetops. It was Myles and his daughter, Rebecca, stopping in for a visit. Myles was happy for us, and agreed to send the Beaver in before the weather turned ugly. With less than an hour of daylight left, they headed for Dease Lake.

Fig 3:
"What a beautiful fat bull he was..."

The next day, we picked up the familiar drone of the Beaver. By the time he had taxied up to shore, the entire camp was packed up and ready for loading. I think a person always experiences mixed emotions when leaving a special place such as this. On the one hand, we are sad about leaving, but on the other is the joy of seeing our children again with all the stories of the hunt. We came back to this lake several times, but like many of life's adventures, the first time was the best.

•••

2

Ida Tours Club Moose...

I wondered how the moose and caribou were handling the heat. Rivers of sweat trickled down my face and chest as we reached the edge of timber line. Another five minutes, and we would be on a low tundra covered ridge, where a fairly stiff breeze was blowing. Ida was ready to collapse by the time we hit the crest. We threw down our packs and sank to the soft caribou moss for a well-earned rest. The ravenous clouds of black flies and mosquitoes were finally overpowered by the wind, so we had a chance to sit back and enjoy the scenery.

Northern BC was in the midst of an early September heat wave, with numerous forest fires currently sending heavy smoke across the horizon. If the weather didn't soon change, we'd be out of luck as far as shooting a moose went. It wasn't cooling off enough at night to hang the meat. Ida complained about a boot rubbing her ankle, so Dr. Fergie had a quick look at it. She couldn't hide her surprise when I took out my knife and cut a hole in the side of her new boot. End of problem.

I removed my boots and socks and lay back for a most peaceful afternoon siesta. Late in the afternoon it began to cool off a bit, so we pulled on our boots and climbed the rest of the way to the top of the ridge. We found another comfortable vantage point, and stayed until sunset, glassing for game and taking photographs. Although we spotted only a few scattered caribou, it was an afternoon to remember.

Morning found us enjoying breakfast to the serenade of a fine family of loons. One look at the sky told us to prepare for another scorcher. I got out my telephoto lens and amused myself as the sun first hit our camp. Nothing is quite as striking as the colours of arctic birch in the fall. Another eye-catcher is the balsam tree with its sticky little purple cones sitting up on top of the limbs like perky little birds.

Shortly after sunrise, a young bull moose walked down to the shore and swam across the narrows just down from camp. He would have been good eating, but we needed a bigger bull to last us all winter. Our kids were growing fast and many of their friends, whose parents didn't hunt, liked to have dinner at our place at every opportunity.

I tried fishing for grayling, but even that was slow. We threw our gear into our little Zodiac and headed for the north end of the lake. A cow moose was feeding quietly in a shallow bay as her calf walked along the shore, seemingly without a care in the world. We pulled our raft up into the low brush and headed up the flat open valley at a nice easy pace.

Along a well-used game trail were the tracks of moose, caribou, grizzly and wolf. A few miles up the valley, we found the perfect place for a mid-day snooze—a nice little hill with a good view, a warm breeze, and no blackflies or mosquitoes.

An hour into our siesta, the heat became unbearable. The weather was better suited for swimming than moose hunting. Yes, swimming, I thought, and as we marched back to camp, I couldn't believe how clever I was. Back in camp, it was cooler on the little sandy beach, where the bottom dropped off quite steeply.

Off with the laundry, and with very little pomp and ceremony, I made the most spectacular dive into this charming lake. Immediately on surfacing I found a blood-curdling scream was in order, but difficult to accomplish. I was paralyzed from my toe-jam up. As I made my way to shore, my lovely wife was standing there in her birthday suit. She said, "How's the water honey?"

I replied, "Wow, fantastic! The deeper you go the warmer it gets!" That was all it took. My lovely trusting bride took the fatal plunge.

The situation suddenly became very grave for me. The cute little French lady transformed into a wild-eyed snarling animal, bent on doing me grievous harm. By the time she got to shore I had explained to her, in no uncertain terms, how much I loved her, and it seemed everything was forgiven. Actually, the worst was yet to come. After lathering up, we needed to rinse off with several pails of pristine northern ice water.

Feeling much refreshed from our little dip, we decided it was time for dinner and tea on the beach. A slight breeze was beginning to pick up out of the west. It looked like a weather change in the making. By daylight, waves were lapping against the shore signaling cooler weather. Breakfast was very casual, as we didn't want to push the hunting effort too much.

With breakfast dishes cleaned up, we relaxed by the shore enjoying a final cup of coffee. Suddenly, a faint droning noise drifted in and out with the breeze, then settled into the very distinct sound of a Cessna aircraft. Within seconds, a sleek red and white 180 powered 172 dipped a wing then circled downwind for a landing.

The plane had brought our good friends, Jim and Lucy Wood, from Terrace, BC, on their annual moose hunt. Every fall, they fly a comfortable camp into the bush, relax, and hunt for a few days, then fly the whole shebang out to Dease Lake. From there, Lucy would load all the meat and gear into the pick-up and head for Terrace. Jim would phone for weather reports and, if all was well, be on his way home. Jim's relaxing trip would take about two hours, and Lucy's rough and dusty one, about seven. Now there's a good woman.

Fig 4:
"That was all it took. My lovely trusting bride took the fatal plunge…"

During their short visit, we caught up on news from the past year, and had a few laughs. I decided that we should be camped at a higher lake, so I asked Jim to send the BC-Yukon pilot in, if he was on his way out empty. Without further ado, they were back in their plane, and we were treated to a signature 'Jim Wood take-off'. A few hours later the BC-Yukon Beaver landed. The pilot said "Have your gear ready, I'll be back in two hours."

Sure enough, two hours later we threw our gear into the Beaver, and were on our way. A short flight north-east and we tossed our little camp out on the shore of a tiny lake high in a mountain basin. Within a few minutes, the Beaver was off and the basin fell silent again. A small creek about two feet wide, trickling out of the lake, was the only sound to be heard.

Situated well above the timberline and a mile from the nearest tree, we felt a sense of urgency on the chill air. Near the creek, and slightly hidden behind a low ridge was a flat grassy spot for our tent.

With our tent set up and everything safely stowed inside, I put my fly rod together to try for a grayling. These hardy little fish can be very finicky in the wind, but when the water goes flat calm they'll swing into action all over the lake. My problem was the constant breeze that was producing a lively chop on the surface. I left my rod standing near the shoreline, cradled in the fork of a stunted willow, and crawled inside the little tent to warm up. It was quite a contrast from yesterday at the ol' skinny dippin' beach.

As we relaxed in the warm tent, I thought about what great adventure was waiting for us. My gut feeling warned me to rest and prepare for a big day. Ida slept quietly beside me, as I lay there watching the tent shake from side to side in the breeze. Then as if by magic, the wind suddenly quit. I rushed out of the tent and ran to my fly rod. A quick cast and a fat grayling was doing his best to skid me into the lake. Three more casts and four sparkling blue grayling were cordially invited to dinner. The wind stopped only long enough to change directions, and was soon blowing from the opposite direction, and the fish quit feeding.

Ida peeled the potatoes while I got to work filleting fish. Our two-burner propane stove was flashed into action and a gourmet meal was in the making. As we sat back and enjoyed the meal, I couldn't help but feel just a little bit lucky. Here we were, out on the tundra, with a belly full of good food, fresh air and mountains all around us, and only wildlife for neighbours.

Gazing casually across the slope behind camp, I caught a trace of movement. There was one of our neighbours, right there about a half mile from the tent. He was a fine looking gentleman too, as he rolled huge boulders down the mountainside in his search for marmots.

I passed the bino's to Ida and it took just one quick glance for her to get that wild, 'get me out of here' look on her face. I explained to her that this old grizzly was slowly working his way around the mountain, and would likely be on the other side by dark. We sat back on a low, moss-covered ridge and glassed the entire basin and beyond, for the rest of the evening. Ida kept a close eye on the bear while I spotted a few scattered caribou on the high slopes, and the odd moose far down in the valley. Finally, the light faded and we retreated to our warm little tent. The trickling sounds of the creek put me to sleep in record time, as my wife lay there with her eyes wide open, waiting for the attack.

Morning found us alive and rested. I quietly got dressed and crawled out into a beautiful frosty morning. Glassing all around camp produced nothing, so I flashed up the coffeepot while Ida dressed.

After a quick breakfast of oatmeal, we loaded up our packs with camera gear, meat bags, water and snacks, and headed for a high wide pass to the west. Our plan was to try for a bull caribou up high, or a moose near one of the lakes down near the timberline.

We slowly made our way up the side of the basin, and into the mouth of the pass, where I began to power out. Still recovering from a battle with hepatitis the winter before, I found it quite a chore climbing at this altitude. Ida took the pack and left me with just the rifle and bino's. Another short burst, and I was out of steam again. This time she took the twelve and a half pound rifle. It is so long, that while hanging from the pack, the butt occasionally hits the side of her knee. She looked like a little slave girl loaded down with all my gear, and there's the big tough guy, dragging his sorry tail along the mountainside, carrying nothing but his bino's.

Another hour, and we were high on the south side of the pass, looking down into a big valley to the west. Within minutes, we spotted several cows and calves, and one big bull moose in the valley bottom. The bull was feeding only a stone's throw from the shore of a big lake. The wind was perfect, sending big waves pounding on the beach. We watched him through the spotting scope until he bedded down about mid-day, at the base of a low rocky ridge.

I sat back and said, "Well Honey, what do you think? He's five miles from camp, but less than a hundred yards from the lake. We can have him cut up and stacked by the lake by 5:00 PM, but it'll be a long uphill hike back to camp."

She sat there for a while, looking at the three miles of arctic birch between the lake and us. "Let's go!" the lady said, and we were off like a pair of hungry wolves.

Our descent started out on a fairly gentle slope near the top of the mountain, and became gradually steeper as we cautiously made our way down to the summit of the pass. Part way down the steepest section, I stopped to give my knees a break, and let Ida catch up. As she is extremely nervous on steep ground, I contemplated rolling her down the rest of the way so we could make better time. After a very short discussion of the subject, I discovered that not giving her a gun or knife was a wise decision on my part.

A quick squint at the bull told us he was on his feet and moving again. Our worries were for naught. He had simply become too warm in the direct sun, and moved into the shade of a stunted spruce. Finally in the pass, we hit an outfitter's horse trail, and the pace picked up considerably. Twenty minutes later we stood just above the first stunted balsam and arctic birch. Something else caught my eye — blueberries, millions of them. Suddenly the moose hunt lost its urgency, and we loaded up on 'bear feed'. These little bushes grow right along the ground, and grow the sweetest of all blueberries.

Finally, all berried up, we checked on the bull one last time, and dropped down on to the wide, sparsely timbered bench land. The horse trail forked about half way across, so we took the right hand trail to the north. Within twenty minutes, we were moving quietly along the south side of the low ridge that ran past the bedded bull. From a few hundred yards downwind, I tried to spot him, but the sun was too bright, and the shadows too dark. We could only hope that he was still there as we slowed the pace and closed to within fifty yards of his hidden bed. Try as I might, I could not see a trace of this guy.

Nearing desperation, I moved along until I was directly across the ridge from the tree which we thought the bull was bedded under. We were, by then, about one hundred yards from the pounding waves, and less than one hundred feet from the tree. I carefully crawled on my belly through a narrow gap in the arctic birch to the crest, dragging my rifle and pack frame behind. The wind was really smoking by now, and the brush was waving wildly around, so I was not concerned about noise. Knowing how well a big bull moose can hide in minimal cover, I just lay there and studied every inch of the area. Suddenly, a lazy groan drifted from the dark shadows directly in front of me. Then I spotted what looked like part of a nose. I brought my bino's up slowly and focused on him. As if by magic, the entire bull took shape, seemingly out of nowhere. The sudden adrenaline rush was almost too much. I'm positive the bull could hear my heart pounding. He was bedded with his back to me, and facing to the left.

I motioned to Ida to get down and crawl up beside me. As she quietly slid in beside me, she whispered "Is he there?"

I whispered "Yep, he's right there in front of us."

I watched her eyes as she tried to spot him. She was looking too far over.

"Honey," I whispered, "look right here, about seventy feet below us."

I could have knocked her eyes off with a stick. Her mouth was hanging open, and her lips were moving, but she couldn't speak. I gave her the bino's so that she could have a better look. She studied him for a while and looked at me and whispered, "My God, he's huge!"

I nodded my head, "Yep, he is, and our work is about to start, so let's just relax, and enjoy this for a while." After a few minutes I slid the .243 into position and placed the cross hairs about six inches behind his ear. It looked good so I carefully eased the safety off, start the squeeze, and 'bang'.

It's hard to describe the feeling that comes over you when you kill an animal. One emotion is certainly relief at knowing your family will eat well over the winter. Cautiously, we made our way down to the bull. He was lying in a big moose-sized hole, about three feet deep. It was going to be an ugly job, so we got with the program immediately.

A few photos, and the work began. Fortunately, we carried lots of rope; we would need lots of it to hold the big bull's legs back out of the way.

After a four-hour struggle, the meat was in a big pile, with plenty of big sticks between all the pieces to facilitate cooling. We piled the meat a little way from the gut pile, in case a grizzly showed up. I left my customary booby trap at the meat pile, my sweaty underwear, hanging from a stick. (I've never lost any meat yet.)

We were too played out to carry the meat to the lake; it would have to wait until we arrived with the Beaver. Not wanting to carry the pack and camera gear five miles back to camp, we threw a rope over a branch and hoisted it into a tree.

With one last look around, I slung the .243 onto my shoulder and headed for the high pass, with my little wife following ... It was already 7:00 PM. A short way up the trail we found a steaming pile of Moose droppings. I stopped and said one word, "Moose!"

A little further on we crested a low ridge, and there he was, standing broadside, looking at us, about eighty yards away. He looked like the

Fig 5:
"The bull was lying in a big moose-sized hole, about three feet deep."

twin of the one we had just bagged. What a sight he was as he trotted off, with his muscles rippling in the sun, and nearly sixty inches of rugged armor sitting atop his head. This guy was already out of velvet, and ready to meet the 'ladies'.

We pushed hard along the flat to try and make up some time. At the blueberry patch, we grazed for a while, then began the slow climb over the pass. The first two hours were brutal, and then we began to break over the top. An hour from camp it turned nearly black dark. We could faintly make out part of our little lake in the distance.

In the daylight, tundra is wonderful to walk on, but in the dark it's full of rocks, grassy mounds, and deep water-filled holes. I found every single one, and the closer to the lake we got, the worse they got. We finally rolled into camp at 11:30, too tired to eat. We just fell into bed and slept in our blood-soaked long johns.

Just after daylight, Ida crawled out of the tent to go to the lady's room. I thought that she either couldn't find it or it was occupied because she crawled right back in.

"Honey! There's a whole herd of caribou outside the tent!" she said, with that sexy morning sleep still stuck in the corners of her big brown eyes.

That did it: now I had to go to the boy's room. Grabbing my rifle I flew out of the tent in my bare feet and bloody long johns. Sure enough, we were surrounded by ladies and children. There was not a bull in the bunch. This was not surprising, as the rut was still two weeks away. Back into the tent we went, and slept for a few more hours.

With the plane not expected for one more day, we had plenty of time to take a dishpan bath, and change our clothes. We stayed around camp and watched all day for a bull caribou to come over the horizon, but it didn't happen.

On the final day, we had camp packed up and piled on shore by mid-morning. Just as well, for it was not long before the familiar drone of IGF broke the silence. Ten minutes after he had landed we were loaded up and headed around the mountain to pick up our winter meat at the big lake.

After about twenty minutes of frantic meat packing, we were off the big lake pointed toward Dease Lake.

This was the first of many moose hunts Ida would make with me. I don't know too many ladies who could put up with as much hardship as she has, and never complain. I may keep her around.

•••

3
Solo for Stones: The First Sheep Hunt...

It was a hot and humid afternoon as I sat in the Kitimat Hospital examining room of Dr. Dave Kuntz. We had just come to the conclusion that I would need back surgery to repair damage sustained in my wild cowboy days.

"You'll need to lose a little weight," he said, "and get your cardiovascular up to snuff in order to speed up your recovery."

I got a silly little grin on my face and replied: "Don't worry Dave, I'll be in shape, trust me." All the while he gave me this skeptical 'Oh sure, I just bet!' look.

"So," he said, "let's pick a date. I'm booked solid until after August 1st. How about August 15th?"

"Perfect," I responded. "Expect to see me about 15 pounds lighter." He gave me the look again.

On the way back to Stewart, I stopped in Terrace and picked up a supply of freeze-dried food and trail mix. "Stand back boys, I'm goin' sheep huntin'!"

The last two weeks before the hunt, I had my gear laid out on the floor so I could see it all. I sat there and tried to imagine every scenario that might befall me. Never having been on a sheep hunt before, I was in something of a quandary about a few things, one of them being where to go. The other problem was that my chosen hunting partner for this trip, Dodd Hareuther, had just suffered a severely crushed hand in a nasty work-related accident. Since good sheep hunting partners are hard to find, I decided to go it alone. As to where to go, I was in the dark; veteran sheep hunters don't reveal their secret places to just anyone.

Four days before opening day (August 1st), I gave Ida and the kids a hug and kiss and set out on the long, dusty journey to Dease Lake. The five-hour drive gave me plenty of time to think about a lot of things, including life in general. I thought about Dodd lying in the Stewart Hospital loaded up on morphine with his hand in ice, swollen up like a football. He was terribly upset as he lay there waiting for transfer to Terrace and, ultimately, surgery. I thought about Ida. She would worry herself sick about me being alone in the mountains. Our three children were still too young for a hunt of this magnitude, otherwise I wouldn't be alone.

Aconversation with a Telegraph Creek native Indian a few years back suddenly crossed my mind. We had landed on the subject of sheep hunting, and subsequently on to his younger years working as a guide for various outfitters across the North. Distinctly recalling the name of a lake he had mentioned, I swung my pick-up over into a rest area and pulled out one of my recently purchased topographical maps. There it was, tucked up against the rugged Coast Mountain Range of northwestern BC. I somehow came to the conclusion that this wild and very remote lake would become my destiny.

Arriving in Dease Lake in mid-afternoon, I was pleased to note a very strong high-pressure system firmly in place. BC-Yukon's famous Beaver, IGF, was shuttling excited hunters and their gear out to their secret sheep patches in the surrounding mountains. Since they were all headed east and I was hell-bent on heading west, a small question kept bothering me: what do they know that I don't?

Then another problem raised its ugly head. After a quick visit with the base manager, I discovered that my flight would cost over $600. While sitting around watching flights come and go, I struck up a conversation with a group of sheep hunters from Cranbrook, BC. They were undecided as to where they wanted to hunt. One of them suggested that possibly I could fly in with their group and save us all some money, since payment was by the mile, not by the person. As a group, we decide that further dialogue was necessary, so we retired to the peace and solitude of the Tanzilla Pub in beautiful downtown Dease Lake.

Finding a table in the noisy milling crowd was quite a challenge. After a while, we found one, rounded up a few chairs, kicked a few broken beer glasses out of the way and settled in for the afternoon. Damn, I love that place.

After several dozen beer and plenty of lively conversation, punctuated by the odd fistfight, we came to the conclusion that we still didn't have the foggiest idea where to go. I slept really well that night for some reason.

Shortly after sunrise, over coffee, the BC-Yukon base manager said "We've got about a four hour break after this next flight if you've made up your mind about where you want to go. With opening morning two days away I decided, Yep, let's do it! I pointed to my secret spot on the map, wrote him a cheque and headed out the door to unload my pick-up.

Now the anxiety attack began, as I sat on my small pile of gear on the dock listening for the Beaver to return. Hopefully, I hadn't forgotten anything, because soon it would be too late to worry about it.

Back in the office, I heard on the radio: "IGF landing in five." Out the door I went and there he was, on final approach for landing, just above the eastern horizon. Within a few minutes, he'd made a beautiful glassy water landing close to the shoreline and was drifting in alongside the dock. I grabbed the wing strut and pulled straight back until the float came to rest against the dock bumpers.

The pilot door opened and out shone the smiling face of Cameron Widrig, a fine young bush pilot and a magnet to gorgeous women. Along about then, proof of his latter quality came strolling down the hill in all her morning splendour. Laurel was Cameron's lovely bride-to-be.

After exchanging greetings, Cameron said "We've got a little time, Fergie, let's have a coffee." Over coffee and a few laughs, we decided that Laurel should fly with us since it was a beautiful day and the Beaver would be nearly empty anyway.

At this point, I will point out that Cameron, back in his late teens, had guided hunters for his grandfather, the famous George Dalziel, founder of Dalziel Hunting Ltd.

With coffee and a quick snack out of the way and my gear stowed in the Beaver, we were ready to fly. Cameron pushed the Beaver away from the float and jumped onto the float as Laurel and I fastened our seatbelts. Within five minutes, we were airborne and pointed west. Another ten minutes, and we were trimmed out at our cruising altitude. The roaring engine made talking nearly impossible.

We flew without conversation for the next hour over some of the most pristine wilderness in North America. Not a mark left by man could be seen anywhere, as we passed over mile after mile of tundra and scattered patches of stunted balsam.

On some of the prominent ridges we spotted small herds of caribou in their dark chocolate summer coats. Later in the day when the black flies became unbearable, they would all move onto some of the many snow patches piled up by the last winter's winds. It was sometimes comical to see fifteen or twenty caribou all trying to stand on a tiny patch of snow at the same time.

Cameron had a map on his lap and scanned the horizon. We must have been right on course, as he stowed it back in the door pocket and continued looking out his side window. As I monitored our progress, looking forward past the propeller, I couldn't help but notice the towering ice covered peaks of the Coast Range.

Just the very thought of trying to fly among them must make a pilot shudder. Thankfully, my trip would end just short of those rugged peaks.

Finally, Cameron nudged me and pointed to a series of more rounded mountains to our right. "There is likely where you'll find a ram," he yelled over the engine noise. Now I was trying to get a fix on the terrain I'd be walking over for the next nine days. Sheep country always looks easier from the air.

Cameron throttled back a little, and through a narrow pass I spotted our landing site, milky blue glacial water stretching for twelve miles north to south. We made a wide swing over the lake, searching for a site for my base camp. A long, sandy beach along the eastern shore looked just right as Cameron throttled back some more and gave her a few degrees of flap. The more elevation we lost, the higher my sheep mountain seemed to get. By the time we touched down it looked like a two-day hike to timberline.

As we drifted into the beach, I could sense the excitement in Cameron. He would have liked to just tie up the Beaver and climb up the mountain with me. Once infected with the sheep fever, you never lose it.

A mild crunch came from the floats as we slid to a halt on the fine gravel. Everyone got out for a well-deserved stroll in the sun. About fifty yards down the beach was the first sign of bears: a rubber raft torn to shreds. For some reason, bears absolutely delight in playing with all things rubber.

Shortly, with all my gear piled on the beach, Cameron and Laurel were ready to go. We floated the Beaver and I held her away from the beach until she flashed up. As they taxied away, I grabbed my spin casting rod and cast directly into the prop wash about fifty feet behind the Beaver. At the very instant he came on to the throttle, a fat two and a half pound lake trout nailed my lure and my hat blew off into the sand. All kinds of action!

After a short battle I 'bonked' my first lake trout. Finding a nice spot on the beach, I took the classic 'fishing pole and fish' photograph.

By this time, it was nearing mid-day and not having eaten yet, I decided to treat myself to a hearty meal. Hooking my propane stove together, I put my largest pot on with about two inches of water in it. Next, I opened the lid on a can of beans and set it in the pot. Then I peeled two big potatoes and threw them in the pot with the bean can. Now the lid went on the pot and out came the ol' moose guttin', wolf skinnin', toothpick makin', fish filletin' knife. Now that's one hell of a knife!

When the potatoes were nearly done, the pot was set on the beach where they would continue to cook in the hot water. The frying pan swung into action with margarine, salt and lemon pepper. When the trout fillets hit the pan, I was treated to the most incredible smell in the world.

"Damn!" I said to myself, " I wonder what the city people are eating today?"

As I sat back against my pack enjoying my meal, I tried to guess where the nearest human was at that moment. Other than the outfitter's camp at the north end of the lake, probably Telegraph Creek.

Now that I had taken some of the slack out of my skin, the desire to climb the mountain somehow just didn't seem that urgent anymore. I slithered a little farther down onto the sand so my head rested on the pack. Soon, I was put to sleep by the antics of several forty-inch rams jumping over fences.

With eating and snoozing out of the way, I'd run out of excuses. I put my aluminum wash basin on the stove to warm up water for dishes. Just back from the beach were a few young cottonwood trees among the scattered spruce and willow. They would be perfect for hanging my base camp out of reach of the grizzlies. I searched out a short, fat piece of driftwood and secured it to a length of light nylon rope. Throwing it up and over a high, stout branch, I was ready to hoist my gear.

By then the water was hot. I washed the dishes and set them on a log to dry as I hoisted my propane tank and stove into the tree. Tying it off securely as high as I could reach, I cut off the remaining rope, fastened on the chunk of driftwood and threw it over another stout branch.

Lastly, I hoisted the remainder of my base camp into the other tree and I was ready to go — sort of.

As a rookie sheep hunter, I hadn't yet discovered some of the wonderful lightweight gear available to the backpack hunter. Here is a list of some of the heavier items that were in my pack:
- Estwing hatchet
- Canon AE1 camera
- Vivitar Series 1 70-210 zoom lens
- Bushnell Spacemaster II spotting scope
- Tripod
- Binoculars
- Super 8 movie camera
- Coleman single burner stove
- Sleeping bag and light mat

- Two-man mountain tent
- Seven freeze-dried meals
- 15 oz. pickle jar of water
- Three pounds of trail mix (granola, mixed nuts and raisins)

All this gear was stuffed into a cruel beat up old Trapper Nelson backpack. Before leaving Stewart, after my pack was loaded, it tipped the scale at 87 pounds. Add my 13 pound custom-built .243 to that and I would carry a 100-pound load up the mountain. If Dodd had been there with me instead of in the hospital with a broken front leg, my pack would only weigh about 60 pounds.

Of one fact I was positive: if I survived this trip at all, I would arrive for my back surgery with a strong heart.

After a short walk around to make sure I'd left nothing behind, I struggled into my pack, hung my rifle sling over the top horn of my pack frame, and staggered off into the timber. The first hour was a tangled nightmare of willows, alder and twisted spruce. The possibility of surprising a bear was nil with all the cussing and crashing as I forced my way through the jungle.

Finally, about the time I was ready to cut my own throat, I broke out onto something of a ridge. I found a good spot to sit without removing my pack. It was 6:00 PM. Suddenly, I was set upon in earnest by millions of black flies and mosquitoes. Now that I'd quit cussing, I guess they thought it was safe to attack. They didn't seem to mind standing up to their knees in sweat as they chewed on my sorry hide.

With several pounds of flesh and blood removed, I felt much lighter. As I plugged along, I wondered what makes a person want to do this to himself. By 8:00, I was still in thick spruce timber and out of water. Every time I stopped to rest, the bugs seemed to multiply. I hadn't had this much attention in ages.

By 9:00, a few balsam were showing up amongst the spruce and the air was finally cooling off. Soon, the spruce trees petered out and the balsam began to open up into lush green, mountain vegetation. The cool fresh smells were almost pungent; such a contrast to the dry, hot spruce slopes below.

Now I was hunting for water. The balsam became more scattered and stunted among brilliant patches of alpine flowers. I could see the mountains directly to the north and south as I broke into the pass to the east. The ground was beginning to level off when I finally heard a trickle of water. Another fifty yards and I found a little pool about two feet across with just a trace of current flowing through it.

That was it. I'd camp there tonight. It was 10:00 PM, an hour of daylight left, and I was played out. After taking on about five gallons of water, I set my tent up and threw my gear inside. The bugs were quite serious about eating what was left of me, so I crawled inside the tent and zipped it up. Now the shoe was on the other foot. With my damp socks in hand I proceeded to swat the stuffing out of the five thousand or more critters who had crowded into the tent with me.

At last, after five hours of sheer misery, I could relax. As I lay there on my bed, the bugs were buzzing furiously only inches from my face. "Too bad, guys, the meat counter is closed 'til morning."

Following a completely uneventful night, I woke up some time around sunrise, which was about 4:30 am this time of year. My blood-thirsty little friends were patiently waiting for me as I slid into my damp clothes. Until then I hadn't noticed how tender my shoulders and feet were. With only two miles to go, part of it very steep, I decided to take it a little easier.

Within minutes, my pack was loaded, my water bottle full, and my screaming, bloodthirsty entourage was pumped and ready. For the first little burst, the weight of the pack on my sore shoulders nearly brought tears to my eyes. Not a lick of pity did I get from the bugs as I picked my way through the knee-high, dew-soaked flowers.

Gradually, as I crested a low rise, I was treated to a beautiful sight — flat ground! I'd reached the summit of the pass at last. Lush vegetation from the shaded slopes gave way to grassy meadows interspersed with small patches of twisted balsam.

It was nearing mid-morning and the sun was burning off last night's dew. With the rising temperature came a welcome breeze giving me a break from the bugs. After snacking lightly on trail mix all morning, it was time to try some of the freeze-dried food. I found a comfortable spot on the south side of the pass and set up my little Coleman stove. While the water was warming up, I glassed the north side of the pass for rams. Although I didn't spot any, it was not difficult to understand why a band of sheep would be happy here with plenty of water and lush alpine feed.

The water was boiling, so I poured it into the package of beef stroganoff. The lady at the sporting goods store had said: "Oh, it's very tasty; whenever I'm in a rush I simply heat up some water, and bingo instant meal!" I waited the required ten minutes, then dove headlong into my instant meal. There was a long pause, and then I took a quick glance around. Maybe I could find a marmot or skunk to stuff into this mess for flavour. I began to realize why that lady looked so damn miserable: she was dying! There was also not the shadow of a doubt that Dr. Kuntz would be absolutely thrilled with my dramatic weight loss.

31

With lunch out of the way, I lay back in the sun with my boots off and drifted off to sleep. The constant breeze had blown the bugs down into the moss.

Around mid-day, I strolled over to a small spring and took on a belly full of cool clear water. Lounging in the grass by the spring, I studied the steep rocky slope I was about to climb. It looked dry; however, I expected to find water on top, as I had spotted several large snow patches during the flight in.

I forced down a last drink of water, filled up the water bottle and headed for my pack. It was time to muster up a little extra intestinal fortitude. I struggled into my pack thinking to myself: "By God, when that stroganoff kicks in, there'll be a big rooster tail of moss and rocks flying up behind me as I blast over the top!"

Slinging my little popgun over the pack frame, I headed the two hundred yards across the meadow to my pre-selected starting point. Strangely, it seemed a little steeper than it had looked from the other side. C'mon, stroganoff!

After three hours of brutal climbing, I was out of water. Since it takes water to make steam, I was out of that too. The one thing I had plenty of was wind. It must have been blowing fifty miles per hour up top, but without the wind I would have overheated hours before. Every time I stopped to rest I looked for any sign of water on the bench above.

I finally spotted a tiny patch of bright green moss about five hundred yards above, on the edge of what looked to be a bench. Suddenly, I was in stampede mode. An hour later, I was nearly there and the green patch looked more promising as it was at the head of a small gully. The last sixty yards was so steep that nothing was growing on it. The ravens had to fly upside down just to land on it.

Before this last ugly burst, I had a good rest, as there didn't appear to be anywhere to stop between where I was and my oasis on the bench. I decided to go straight up the centre of the gully where there was sound footing. As rested as I was going to get, I headed off up the gully with grim determination. Fifty feet from the top, my legs were burning up and my head was pounding, but I didn't dare stop. I didn't dare look up either, lest I lose my balance. Finally, I was struggling over moist green moss. I lifted my head and stopped. With my head just above the level of the bench, I was looking at twenty-six pairs of very startled stone sheep eyes, less than sixty yards away.

Four more monumental steps and I fell to my knees then to my side. Slowly, I struggled out of the pack straps then rolled, face down, into the sweetest little trickle of water I'd seen in over five hours.

All the while the sheep just stood there staring at me in total amazement. They were all ewes, lambs and a few juvenile rams. Then it dawned on me to get my camera out. As I rummaged through my pack they began to feed slowly away. By the time I got my telephoto lens hooked up they were nearly too far away for good photos.

After another drink of water, I sat back, relaxed and took in the beauty. Off to the right on the far east end of the bench I spotted a few boulders that looked out of place on top of a little knob. I zoomed in with my camera lens and it was rams, two big rams, facing away and a half-curl looking right at me. They were all bedded down within ten feet of each other. I set up the spotting scope and tripod. Once focussed on the rams, I could see, even from three hundred yards away, that the two big guys were legal. They hadn't spotted me yet but the young guy was beginning to hyperventilate. He stood up and tapped one front foot on a rock — the big guys began to pay attention. With a casual glance one of them finally located the source of the young ram's anxiety.

Their next move really surprised me. The two big rams slowly stood up, had a good stretch and, like two retired old gentlemen, headed casually down the trail straight toward me. I was caught a little off guard, but when they moved closer, I swung into action with the telephoto. They seemed to know that sheep season wasn't open yet as they cruised by at less than one hundred yards with the sun shining amber through their horns. Then I remembered the movie camera. Bad news: I had left the only batteries I had in the camera and the power button had been pushed on while in the pack. Live and learn.

It was 5:00, I had nearly five hours to find a suitable site and set up my spike camp. The wind was still blowing hard from the Coast Mountains but so far there was no rain and only scattered clouds. To the north, the ground sloped upward to the top of a high rocky hogback. The east end dropped off into a deep canyon, while the west end sloped off gradually to a little point, then fell steeply off toward the lake. I chose to camp partway up the slope in a little dip about one hundred yards below that little point. This way, I was close to the little spring down on the bench and within twenty minutes of the top of the relatively flat-topped mountain.

I set up my tent on an almost level spot and prepared for another culinary delight. Tonight, I would treat myself to something called beef and rice. This was sure to be a big hit as I am a great fan of anything with rice.

As I prepared to dine, the wind threatened to tear my little tent to shreds. I'd taken the precaution of tying my tent ropes around small rocks, then stacking big rocks on top of the small ones.

Now for dinner. The stuff I was preparing to eat closely resembled a blend of tofu and sawdust. Since stabbing the cook was out of the question I did the honourable thing and choked it down quickly. The good news was that I wouldn't have to do this again until the next night. Possibly by then, I'd have sheep meat to eat.

I decided to use my last three hours of daylight to hike up to the point and take my first peek over the top. About four hundred yards away, up on the high hogback to the right, the two big rams had bedded where they could keep an eye on me. Just before the little point I took my pack off and, dragging it with one hand and cradling my rifle in the other, crawled to the crest.

With my eyes barely above the horizon, I was treated to terrain such as I had never seen before. Except for the high ridge on my right, this end of the mountain was mostly flat or gently sloping ground with low rocky ridges and pillars sticking up everywhere. If it weren't for the abundance of short lush feed growing among the rocks, I would have thought I was on the moon.

An odd formation on the skyline caught my eye. With the help of my bino's I discovered it was a lone ewe. She was about five hundred yards away, bedded on one of the thirty foot high rock pillars. With the tripod and spotting scope set up, I had a closer look. Her lamb could be seen curled up against her, out of the wind. Swinging the scope to the right, I picked up a group of ewes and lambs walking along a flat at the base of the big ridge.

As the sun set beyond the Coast Mountains, the two rams stood up, had a good stretch and fed their way over the high ridge to the east.

Looking back to the west, I found myself suddenly looking into a pair of eyes about one hundred fifty yards away. A big billy goat, on his way up from a side canyon to feed had just spotted me. We must have looked comical staring at each other with only the tops of our heads visible. Through the spotting scope, it was easy to see that this was a record-book goat. His horn length appeared to be well over ten inches with massive bases that nearly touched in the middle.

He studied me for several minutes, then, like a fat old man with sore ankles, picked his way slowly up and over the ridge. As went the sun, so went the heat. The chill wind drove me back into my tent where sleep came easily despite the boisterous wind.

It was just breaking daylight when I crawled out of the tent, pulling my rifle and pack behind me. It was opening day and to say I was 'wired' would have been an understatement. The wind hadn't let up, but the weather was still holding as I made my way in the half-dark toward a spot I had picked the night before. A low ridge two hundred yards beyond where the lone ewe had been bedded, was where I would wait for daylight.

As I crossed a low saddle on the crest of the ridge the wind threatened to blow me into the canyon below. This was where I wanted to wait, but I had to find shelter from the wind. Amongst a huge pile of jagged boulders, I found a hole that I backed into feet first. It was not great, but it would have to do. A few minutes before the sun popped over the eastern horizon, I started taking photos. I was treated to the wildest sunrise I'd seen in years.

For the first time, I could see the north side of the big ridge. As the first sun hit its slopes, I glassed for rams without luck. Slowly, the sun worked its way down into the bottom of the canyon below me. Glassing in the wind brought tears into my eyes. On the far side of the canyon, a band of six ewes and lambs were out on a gentle slope feeding in the sun. West of them, another band of nine ewes and five lambs fed near the head of the canyon. After glassing for half an hour, I was chilled to the bone, so I struck out for the big ridge. I hoped to spot rams below the eastern end out of the wind. I stayed on the north side of the crest, just in case some rams showed up along the rim below where I had first seen them the day before.

I peeked over into the pass from the shade of a huge boulder. Far below and to the right, my little tent was barely visible. Out on the bench, near the spring, nine ewes and four lambs were feeding slowly up toward the tent. If they kept to their course, they'd cross the ridge one hundred yards above it.

To the left and east above them, was the rocky point where I first saw the three rams. From above, I could now make out a very distinct sheep trail. It began up at the rocky point then ran down a long winding hogback toward the bottom and ended up crossing the east end of the pass. Had I known about this trail beforehand, I would have come up that way. Just then, another band of ewes and lambs appeared from behind a patch of scrub balsam near the bottom. They were feeding their way up the ridge, leaving the trail here and there to grab a bite.

This seemed to be a regular sheep highway, and I was camped just out of sight of it. (A few years later, on another hunt, I discovered a large mineral lick near the east end of the pass, explaining the heavy traffic along the trail.) With the wind blowing this hard they were not likely to pick up the scent of my camp from the trail. The sun was beginning to produce a little heat, so I moved to the lee side of a moss-covered hump. From here, much of the eastern slope could be seen, but so far there was no sign of rams.

Far across the big canyon to the north, a mile-wide lower bench ran for four or five miles along the eastern slope of a round-topped mountain. Though the heat waves were getting bad, I could see a few small bands of ewes and lambs far out on the flats. A pack of wolves would have had a fine picnic out there.

About face and looking across the pass to the south, I could see several fairly prominent sheep trails resembling light thread laid neatly along the contours of the mountainside. If I was patient and sat here long enough, I was surely going to see rams on one of these trails.

It was time to check the bench below camp. The two bands of ewes had joined forces and were all bedded around the spring. The ewes were contentedly chewing their cud and the lambs were all ironed out flat in the sun. They had the right idea. I arranged my pack behind me and kicked back for a quiet siesta.

By midday, nothing had moved, so I decided to amuse myself with my macro lens. Through the lens, I discovered a seldom seen world of beauty and perfection nestled among the rugged boulders. All around me were tiny mountain flowers and brightly coloured lichen. And yet, in only five months the top of this ridge would be one of the most inhospitable places on earth.

Late afternoon, and all the ladies and children were up feeding, but still no rams. I had moved along, below the skyline, to the west end of the big ridge. The wind was still raging, but at least it was bearably warm as I lounged amongst a pile of comfortable boulders.

It was time to plan my strategy for the next morning. I didn't expect to find rams with the ewes, but with ewes all over the top of the mountain, I wondered where a ram would find privacy. I suspected they were hanging around some of the many canyons below the plateau. According to my map, there were a few rugged canyons just north of camp, on the west-facing slope above the lake.

I had a commanding view from my lofty perch of a big chunk of sheep country. Small bands of sheep appeared, feeding in every direction. The temperature was dropping fast and still no rams. By sunset, the nursery crowd from the spring was on its way — right up the sheep highway above my tent. They couldn't see it and certainly didn't appear to scent it. I maintained my cold vigil until nearly dark, then worked my way cautiously down the ridge towards camp.

Dinner, for some reason, went down a little easier that night. Before going to bed, I made one last trip out of the tent to water the flowers and there, sixty yards above on the horizon, stood a very surprised half-curl ram. Were the big guys with him? I'd never know, but at least there was hope for tomorrow.

Daylight found me posted at the lookout point, patiently glassing around for rams. I munched away on trail mix with my back to the wind. A casual glance far down the slope toward the lake revealed a young ram. Out came the spotting scope. He was probably the same half-curl and feeding just across the little canyon the big billy had come from. Beyond the ram, about three hundred yards, the slope curved around to the right and out of sight. About the same distance above him, the mountain was flat but for a few humps and rock pillars. I intended to stick my nose over that side, but first, the big canyon to the north needed a quick squint.

On the way over to the north canyon, I bumped right into a big band of ewes, fifteen or twenty of them, as I rounded the corner of a low rocky ridge. They were only a short stone's throw away but after running less than fifty feet, they just stood there, wide-eyed, and watched me walk by. Twenty minutes of glassing at the north canyon turned up only more ewes.

I set off to see if the half-curl had any tutors. Two rocky pillars stood at the edge of the drop-off were where I was headed. Twenty minutes later, after running into more ewes, I glassed the steep western slope overlooking the lake. All I saw was the little ram bedded by himself.

There was a heavily used sheep trail back from the edge and parallel to the big slope It led to the first big canyon that ran toward the lake. Nearing the edge, I slowed down and glassed everything carefully. Finally, I was looking down into a wild and unstable looking mess. The creek bottom appeared to drop off a cliff on the lake side. The upstream side was very rough and steep at first, then petered out into a high pass to the east.

Further glassing revealed a few more ewes and lambs along the canyon walls, but still no rams. The trail dropped straight off the edge and angled slightly upstream over loose boulders and rubble. It looked rough, but away I went. In the creek, bottom I took on a little water and munched on some trail mix before tackling the steep climb out the other side. There in the creek bottom the sheep smell was almost sickening, even in the wind.

Twenty minutes later, with my temperature gauge in the red, I broke out onto another flat bench. As with the other side of the canyon, the big round mountain rose to the east and the bench dropped off sharply to the lake on the west.

Half a mile away, on the very edge of the bench, stood a series of rock pillars resembling old broken totem poles. I headed for their shelter, as the wind was really howling on the open bench. Generations of stone sheep must have had the same idea, because I soon discovered a solid row of sheep beds along the lee side of the pillars.

As the chill wind picked up even more velocity, sinister black storm clouds began to force their way over the Coast Range out of the Gulf of Alaska. My beloved high-pressure system was losing ground fast. The next canyon was only a twenty-minute hike to the north, but my survival instinct told me to line out for camp.

Fifteen miles to the west, the jagged peaks had ripped the guts out of the storm. As the first curtains of rain advanced down the distant mountainside, I left the cover of the pillars on a forced march for camp.

Shortly after entering the first canyon, I came abreast of a fifty-foot wide rockslide. I'd entered the canyon too low down. On the other side of the slide, I could see part of the sheep trail. To get around the top of this mess would take me twenty minutes. Against my better judgement, I looked for a way across. A few large slabs of rock would make good stepping stones, but I'd need to be on the dead run all the way across. I marked every step, took a deep breath, and away I went. By the time I gained solid ground on the other side, I was afraid to look back. It sounded like the whole mountainside had let go.

Safely back on the trail, I looked back at a roaring, popping river of rock as it spilled over a cliff into the canyon bed, one hundred yards below.

By the time I topped out on the south side, the rain was less than five miles away and I still had two miles to go. I must have been quite a sight as I speed-walked my way along the narrow trail.

Finally, I was standing on the little point in the raging wind, looking down on my tent. What a welcome sight! The first heavy drops smacked the side of my face while I unzipped the tent and slid my rifle and pack inside.

The unbridled fury of the storm was showing no mercy on my flimsy little tent as I warmed a pot of water for dinner. The wall facing the storm was bowed in and the other was bulging out. This had to be the most fun I'd had since the pigs ate my cousin.

The storm raged on for three hours, then, just before dark, the wind slowed down and the water shut off. Out of the tent I went, into a strange

and suddenly quiet world. The tail end of the storm was already depart-
ing to the east, leaving a few patches of blue sky in its wake.

I made my way down to the spring in the fading light for a nightcap.
The rain had enhanced the already rich smells of the mountains. Over a
cool drink of water, I sat and reflected on the past few days. I was having
a great time in spite of some of the hardships, but how was I ever going to
describe this adventure back home without missing a few special mo-
ments like this?

Back in the tent, stretched out in my down bag, I stared up at the peak
of the tent as I planned the next day's adventure. This time, I would hunt
the big bench across the north canyon. According to the map, I would be
in for a long hike, so I'd need to be on the move by daylight, which was
about 3:00 am. This left me with only about four hours to sleep, so I got
with the program.

The big drink of water before bed got me up right on time the next
morning. Within ten minutes, I was on my way to the little point.
In the faint morning light, I saw nothing close by, so it was off to the
ridge overlooking the north canyon.

By the time I reached the ridge, the sun was nearly above the horizon.
Across the canyon, a dozen ewes and lambs fed on the gentle slope just
back from the canyon's edge. Behind them, to the north, the
snow-capped mountain resembled the top of a big mushroom. I hoped to
find a ram on its north slope.

Having glassed all I could see from there, I headed west to cross the
top end of the north canyon. In less than half an hour, I was following a
well-used sheep trail along the north side. I could see the rugged slopes
and cliffs below the ridge that I had glassed from at sunrise. A ram down
in this canyon was in no danger from man or beast. As I scanned the
many feed patches and bedding areas below, the constant popping and
rattling of moving rock reached my ears.

I continued along the trail, below the low ridge that the ewes were
feeding on earlier. I was still in the shade when, only thirty yards above
on the skyline, I spotted the horns of a ewe sticking up. Crouching down,
I moved closer, then slowly stood up.

There, lying facing the sun and chewing her cud, was Ms Sheep in the
company of last year's and this year's lambs. With the bino's refocused
for close range, I studied them carefully. In the bright morning sun the
old girl's eyes sparkled like marbles and her horns were a glowing amber.
The yearling's eyes were closed as she soaked up the meagre heat. The
little white lamb, on the other hand, was curled up tight against the
shady side of his mother with his eyes closed.

A slight breeze was blowing, but it was in my favour. Crouching down again, I quietly lay my rifle down and took off my pack. Now, with just the bino's, I crawled to within twenty yards. If I were a wolf, I'd have been drooling all over myself. The ewe now closed her eyes so I stood bolt upright, facing into the sun.

At this point, the lamb opened his eyes and they nearly popped out of his head. He looked at his mom, then back at me. He was in a terrible fix. Here was this horrible, mangy looking varmint ready to eat him, and his mom just lying there with her eyes closed, chewing her cud.

Finally, the trembling lamb got her attention and she turned her head for a look. That did it — all hell broke loose! The ewe leapt straight ahead out of her bed, then turned hard right for the canyon's edge with the lamb scrambling at her side. The yearling panicked and ran up the hill, then turned and ran back past me in great leaping bounds more suited to a mule deer. I was sure they'd all be killed the way they had gone over the edge. But after a quick look down the slope, I was satisfied that they were safe below one of the many rock faces.

The temperature was rising quickly as the sun made its ascent in the east, but to the west was a different picture. Ominous storm clouds were beginning to force their way over the Coast Range.

At first the travelling was easy as I hiked northward along the lower eastern slope of the "mushroom" mountain. Below and to my right, the mile wide bench stretched for five miles to the north then hooked westward into another big canyon.

On a prominent rise I came to a group of boulders that seemed to invite me to rest awhile. It was time for breakfast and a good look at the country ahead.

I took a quick look around and immediately spotted a herd of nine goats two miles to the north — all nannies and kids. They were far out on the flats about half a mile from the edge of the bench. It was obvious that they hadn't been harassed by wolves or bears for awhile. Beyond the nannies, on a rugged knob at the north-east corner of the bench, lay two fat old billies.

This was definitely goat country, so I didn't expect to run into a lot of sheep for awhile. I decided, since I was going in that direction anyway, to see how close I could get to this nursery crowd.

The night's heavy rain had all the little creeks running full. A series of springs along the eastern slope had saturated the gently sloping bench, and big patches of watercress were growing everywhere. A big feed of green salad was in order. This also explained why the goats were so far out on the flats.

They were only a mile away by that time, so I walked straight toward them, trying not to show them any lateral movement. It seemed as though I might end up in the middle of the herd before they spotted me, but finally the nanny on the far left was the first to make the shocking discovery.

Thrown into a complete dither, she bolted in the direction her body was facing, straight up the mountain to my left. Good move — if she ran for seven miles or so in that direction, she'd be safe.

The other ladies discovered me and stampeded for the edge of the bench to my right. By the time they were well under way, the lone nanny above to the left discovered her grave error in judgement and stopped to work on "Plan B". This plan took less than a second to implement, as she launched off down the hill in reckless bug-eyed nanny goat abandon. Nothing is quite as awkward and comical as a mountain goat running on flat ground, except possibly a hunter running in goat country.

I felt sure the next time Ms. Nanny led her happy group out onto the veldt, she'd have a good look around first. Out of curiosity, I took a little detour over to the billy goat point. Though they'd long since departed over the edge in the wake of the nanny stampede, their scent was still holding strong. It was enough to gag a buzzard. I was sure the old gentlemen were directly below me, but the overhanging cliff prevented me from seeing anything except timber 2000 feet below.

Back to the west, black clouds were sliding over the top of the mushroom mountain. I'd need to find a comfortable spot to weather the storm so I headed north toward the big canyon indicated on my map.

Two miles later and half a mile from the canyon, the clouds opened up and let fly. I had mobilized my secret defence system — a six-by-eight foot sheet of heavy plastic. I stood on the end of the plastic, facing into the storm. Then I lay back on the ground, sliding my pack up until my head rested on the top end of it. Next, I pulled the plastic up over my head and tucked it under the top of the pack. With my rifle pulled in against my side, I pulled the sides of the plastic in and tucked them under my hips to keep the wind out. As the storm raged on, I drifted off to sleep under the constant spattering of rain on my warm shelter.

I was roused some time later by the chattering of gophers. The rain and wind had quit and the sun was breaking through. Shaking the water off the plastic, I folded it up and tuck it back in my pack. All around me, on little humps and rocks, gophers were sitting up, warming their fat little bellies in the sun.

Now for a look into the canyon. As I got closer, I saw a solid rock ridge splitting the canyon with a creek running on each side of it. Up the canyon to the south, was a gently sloping bowl with a little pool in the middle of it. In a little green meadow at the outflow of the pool, lay two ewes with young lambs. I was beginning to think that I might never see another ram.

Moving back from the canyon so as not to spook the ewes, I sat and thought about my situation. If I went straight over the pass northwest of the mushroom mountain I'd come out at the first canyon above the lake. If I went back the way I had come, it would take me two hours longer.

Since the climb wasn't too steep, I decided to tackle the pass. But first, I had a plan. I'd be arriving in camp very late, and wouldn't be coming back to this side of the mountain, so I went grocery shopping. Placing my pack over a grassy hump, and lying the .243 across it, I proceeded to gather a few gophers for dinner.

After skinning, cleaning and washing them I stuff them into my top pack. The only wood in miles was stunted wolf willow, so I searched around and filled all my pockets with soggy dead sticks.

About then, another storm decided to strike, but this time I climbed up into a mess of huge boulders and crawled in under one that was overhanging. It suddenly felt a lot colder: it was snowing!

I took out my three gophers and lay them on a rock. Then, I took out the plastic and wrapped it around my legs and hips. I constructed a crude fireplace, got my willow sticks out, and built a little fire. 'Little' was the operative word in this last statement. As soon as the lighter took hold, I got all three gophers over the flame at the same time.

As the snow swirled around, I lay there stubbornly holding my fingers to the fire. "Damn," I thought, "ain't this fun?"

Finally, after smouldering away for ten minutes, the fire burned out. My fingers were barely warm and so, I suspected, were the gophers.

I was wishing Dodd were here to share this special meal. "Oh well," I thought, "I guess I get to enjoy it all by myself." The first bite was a challenge to keep down, but after that it was just like eating Kentucky Fried Chicken. In honesty, it was awful.

The feast and the snowstorm ended at about the same time. With my plastic back in the pack, I headed straight up through the rocks, keeping to the left of the canyon so I could gain altitude faster. Within an hour, the steep slope began to level off a bit as I approached the snow line. Once on the snow, I found the footing was a little more predictable, but the wind was picking up. I wasn't really interested in waiting out a storm up on the snow pack. It was 8:00pm and I was still three hours from camp, so I had to get the best performance possible out of my gophers.

By the time I reached the summit, it was 9:00 PM and blowing violently out of the west. A huge ugly storm was starting across the lake toward me, and would arrive in twenty minutes. I had to get down out of the snow before it hit or I would be in one hell of a fix.

I was beginning to power out, but managed to reach bare rock just as the flakes of snow stung my face. After quickly locating a few nice soft rocks to lie down on, I got safely tucked in under my plastic. In a few minutes I was fast asleep and the storm raged on for over an hour. Some time after it was over, my own snoring woke me. The sky was a little lighter now that the dark clouds had passed, but it was 11:00pm. In half an hour it would be black dark.

Down the slope I went, headed for the southern rim of the first canyon. Soon I was on the sheep trail and pointed for camp. At last, I stood on the little point, but I couldn't see my tent. It was nearly black dark now and as this was the darker side of the ridge, the last one hundred yards down the camp was fairly tricky. Once in the tent, I located my little flashlight and checked my watch. It was nearly midnight and I'd been on the trail for twenty-one hours.

Sunrise found me still in bed. I was a little hungry, so I got out my diminishing supply of trail mix and had breakfast. I wondered if a ram was standing on the hill looking down at the tent. I was too tired to look. In the corner was the last of my grub: one freeze-dried meal and two packets of Lipton's Cup-a-Soup. It was a good thing Dodd wasn't here or I may have had to turn cannibal.

I wasn't going to worry about that until there was something to worry about. Quietly, I unzipped my tent and stuck my head out. It was a beautiful morning. Mornings like this made you glad a bear didn't eat you during the night. On the other hand, if a bear had taken a bite out of me, he'd very likely have spat me out again.

I decided to hike up the ridge and sleep above the sheep highway. I didn't intend to travel too far, as I was a bit "stove-up" from the twelve-mile stroll of the previous day. Twenty minutes later I was parked in a comfortable boulder patch two hundred yards above the sheep trail. I was beginning to think that this was where I should have been all along. From there, at the leading edge of the big ridge, I had a fairly good view of this end of the mountain. After a good look around, and feeling confident that I wouldn't be attacked right away by a band of rams, I lay back in the sun and drifted off to sleep.

As the predictable morning thermals developed, the breeze picked up. More glassing revealed two ewes with lambs, bedded in the sun, near the west bench overlooking the lake. A low, rocky ridge on my side of them would provide cover for a photo shoot. The short hike felt good on my tired bones. Soon, I was in position behind the ridge with the telephoto mounted on my camera. The ladies were completely unaware as I zoomed in and snapped off a few shots. Backing off quietly, I made my way around to the north of the ewes.

I eased past them through a low spot on my way to the two big rock pillars at the edge of the bench. With camera ready, I marched into the open just before the pillars. The ewes, now on my left, jumped up and stared bug-eyed at me as I took a photo. Before they could decide what to do, I turned away and casually strolled to the edge of the bench between the pillars.

The ewes were now more curious than alarmed. As they began to feed, the lambs took advantage of the situation to nurse.

A cautious look over the edge revealed no sheep of any description. Moving back to the ewes' side of the pillars, I found a comfortable spot facing the sun, then took off my rifle and pack. I was soon stretched out on the grass snoozing within eighty yards of two ewes and lambs who were, once again, doing the same.

Toward mid-afternoon, after a peaceful rest, I sat up and had a look around. Once again, all the sheep were doing the same thing. The ewes stood up and stretched, giving me no more than a casual glance as I loaded up and headed off toward the first canyon.

There, on the edge of the canyon, with a few boulders for cover, I decided to spend the rest of the day. Scattered bands of ewes and lambs were feeding in nearly every direction. Many of them knew I was there, but they seemed to know that I presented no danger.

By sundown, I'd seen perhaps sixty sheep but no rams. As I followed the trail two miles back to camp, small bands of ewes raised their heads from feeding to watch me walk by. That night I prepared my last freeze-dried meal. This left me with the two packages of Cup-a-Soup. It looked very much like I'd have to get the preliminaries out of the way and get on with the sheep hunt.

Sometime during the night, it began to rain and I slept peacefully until it suddenly quit and I woke up. Reaching for my flashlight, I looked at my watch. It was 4:00 am, why wasn't it light yet? Quietly, I unzipped the tent and stuck my head out.

Instantly, like a ton of bricks, I was hit by an anxiety attack. I could feel it: something was going to happen. I crawled right out into the wind and had a good look around. It was just starting to turn daylight, but the clouds were black and sinister. Back into the tent I went, and scrambled into my clothes. Within minutes, I was headed up to the lookout point, all the while fearing I might be spotted by rams.

From the point, where it was a little lighter, I spotted a ewe bedded on a knob across the billy goat canyon. I glassed the skyline of the big ridge to the right; there was nothing. For some reason, I was expecting rams to come up the sheep highway from the pass below. My instinct told me to get up into the rocks at the base of the big ridge. I didn't want to spook the ewe away, as I needed her to alert me when the rams showed up.

I was looking for ideas. To the left, down on the lake, a big cloudbank was blowing my way. If it didn't arrive soon, I'd die of hypothermia.

Finally, as the cloud blew between the ewe and me, I got up and scrambled for the rocks. I made it about three hundred yards up the ridge before the cloud petered out and I had to dive behind a rock. At least now I was warmed up and slightly above the big sheep trail as I waited for the next cloud to blow through.

By the time it arrived, I was nearly frozen again. This time, with only two hundred yards to go, I thought I could make it — I didn't. Twenty feet below my perch, the cloud petered out. A quick look at the ewe told me she hadn't spotted me.

Turning uphill, I climbed up into my lair, sat down and checked the ewe again. Good — she was okay.

I needed to try and get comfortable in case I was going to be there awhile. I took out the spotting scope and set it upon the tripod in front of me. My rifle was placed on my right, nose-down in the rocks. My pack was behind my back so I could sit back partly out of the wind and glass for rams.

As I focussed the scope on the ewe, I noticed for the first time her little white lamb curled up against her chest out of the wind. Then, as I was studying her, she suddenly fixed her gaze on something to the north. Well, I was expecting rams from the south, but if they wanted to come from the north, I could accept that.

Following her gaze with the bino's, I spotted movement but couldn't identify it. Switching to the spotting scope, I could make out a sheep head coming up out of the north canyon. It was either a small ram or a big ewe. Right behind came another one the same size.

I was confused. Their horns looked a little too heavy for ewes, and their bodies looked square and blocky like young rams. Then one of them squatted to pee and answered the big question. This brought me to the conclusion that they were likely both barren. As they casually strolled across the flats toward the ewe and lamb, I couldn't help but wonder what their ribs would smell like roasting by a fire.

Clatter! Rattle! Clatter! What the hell? I sat up and looked overtop the spotting scope. I thought I must have been dreaming. Seven rams were marching along the trail from the south as if they were on a mission. Completely unaware of my presence, they sounded like a team of horses pulling a buckboard across the rocky flat. Quickly I got back on the scope and looked at the lead ram — he took my breath away. Then I panned along to the ram bringing up the rear. He was a dandy, too. Back to the lead ram; I decided he was the one I wanted.

I didn't dare move the spotting scope, lest I spook them. Carefully, I pulled my .243 up out of the rocks and fed a shell into the chamber. I was sitting in an awkward position for shooting, but there was little choice as the rams were by then two hundred fifty yards off and angling slightly away.

As I picked the ram up in my scope, I tried to swing with him. I took a deep breath, let it all out and started the squeeze. The cross hairs stayed on him quite well ... Crack! Instantly the ram bolted thirty feet to the right, then stopped and turned to face the other rams. By then I was reloaded, and, Crack! He was down. The other rams milled around him in confusion, but soon realized that danger was somewhere nearby.

I remembered the camera as I poked the rifle back down in the rocks and struggled with the pack. With the camera out, I removed the 35 mm. lens and attached the telephoto. The rams headed for the big ridge behind me. They would pass within fifty yards of me if they didn't pinpoint me first.

The light was poor and my adrenaline was in the red, but I started shooting photos. The new leader heard me advance the film and stopped fifty yards to my right as he tried to locate me. I got two more shots away before he spotted my hiding place and led the other rams up over the top.

Now everything was quiet again but for the wind. I seemed to be in a daze as I slowly put all my gear back in the pack. It was difficult to believe all that had taken place in the past ten minutes.

Hoisting the pack and rifle, I slowly made my way down to the ram. This was a moment I hoped never to forget. I lay the pack and rifle down and walked over to him. Then I got down on my knees and, bending forward, looked into his open eyes. At this moment I was close to tears. Standing up, I walked slowly around him and studied every part of his body. How could such a delicate looking animal survive in such a hard land? For a time I just sat beside him. Finally, I reached over and touched his horn. It was warm, almost hot.

I was in no hurry to do any knife work, so I set up my camera on the tripod and took a few photos. Eventually I had to get started. I first removed the cape, the skin from the head to the ribs, then boned out the back straps and hindquarters. Next came the ribs and fillet. All this was spread out on a meat bag to cool. By that time I was overdue for a drink, so I set out for water at a little spring not far away.

By the time I got back, it was time to load up and head for camp. Halfway to camp, on the sheep trail, I came face to face with an old ewe and her band as they rounded a pillar of rock. They turned and sprinted a short way up the hill, then stopped to look as I got out the telephoto again. I managed to get a good shot as they detoured around the pillar.

Back in camp the stove was soon fired up and 'soup de filet de sheep' was on the way. It was midday, the wind was still fairly brisk, and for now the rain was holding off. While brunch was warming I took the time to unpack the meat and lay it out on a meat bag to crust up and cool out properly. So far, the weather was cooperating quite well.

With lunch out of the way I got to work on the cape, splitting the lips and turning the ears. This little chore took up most of the afternoon, but finally it was all salted down and rolled up in a meat bag inside the tent. To eliminate weight, I took the hatchet and trimmed off any bone and meat not needed on the skull.

Just before dark, as I cooked the last package of soup and some more fillet, two yearling ewes stopped by for a visit. I managed to take three good photos, first on the skyline, then on the slope, as they moved in for a better look only thirty yards from my tent. Before turning in, I bagged up the meat and tucked it under the fly on the down-wind side. If a bear showed up in camp, he'd be in for a wreck.

As I lay there in bed, I thought about all that had taken place in the past week. As a rookie sheep hunter, I suppose I'd done a few things the hard way, but, what the hell, this had been an adventure I wouldn't trade for anything, and it wasn't over yet. Was it possible for the average working man to have a greater adventure than this? I can't say for sure, but all this fun made my belly button nearly touch my backbone. On that note I drifted off to sleep.

Sunshine. I'd slept in until 6:00 am. That was fine; I needed a good rest. In no hurry to move, I just lay there and planned my day. First, I had to unroll the cape and let the water run out of it so it could be re-salted. Then, everything would need to be packed carefully in order that I get it all in my pack.

Fig 6:
"I reached over and touched his horn. It was warm, almost hot."

First, I unzipped the tent and checked the meat; it was okay. A quick squint across the western horizon told me it could get hot. After getting dressed I had breakfast — a big drink of water. Then I spread the cape out flesh-side-up to dry in the sun. Before breaking camp, I set up the camera and tripod for a few photos. I was surely going to miss this spot. By the time the old Trapper Nelson was loaded, I could barely wrestle it into position to climb into. Down the ridge, three hundred yards toward the lake, was a rock I'd be able to sit on with another rock to lean the pack against. I took my rifle down there and leaned it against the bottom rock.

Back at the pack, I lay back in the sun and thought about this little project for awhile. It took fourteen hours to come up the mountain. If I could find a better route down, I hoped to be in base camp in seven or eight hours. It was 9:00 am.

I took one last look around, then sat down in front of the pack and slid into the straps. Then, sliding up until the straps dug down into my shoulders, I slowly leaned forward, tipping the top end of the load onto my upper back and neck. With a huge grunt I staggered to my feet and braced myself as the pack settled into position.

With no time to waste, I turned and made my way toward the rock where I'd take my first rest. I had no idea how much weight I had on but

Fig 7:
"I was surely going to miss this spot..."

it felt like well over two hundred pounds. To balance the load, I had to lean well forward and the weight was squeezing the breath out of me.

At the rock, after carefully sitting down, I was completely winded and wondered, How am I ever going to endure eight hours of this kind of punishment? Maybe I'd get my second wind, and just sprint down the mountain.

I had a short sip from the little water bottle in my coat pocket. Then I reached for my rifle and slid it in position, with the sling hooked over the top right frame of the pack.

Another monumental struggle and I was on my feet and moving again. The side hill gave way to a gentle hogback running parallel to the pass below to my left. Soon, nearly winded again, I was looking for a place to rest. A steep little grassy mound would have to do, as I saw no more rocks between me and the timber six hundred yards below.

As I struggled for wind and had another sip of water, I noticed something about twenty feet away. It looked like the faint trace of a trail. Rejuvenated, I leapt to my feet (in a manner of speaking) and careered off down the horse trail.

Five hours later, after countless rest breaks and stick-my-head-in-the-creek sessions, I staggered out across the beach and into the lake. As my boots filled with soothing water I tried to muster up the courage to tackle the last four hundred yards to base camp. I tried the beach, but it was too soft for good footing, so back into the water I went. The last hundred yards was brutal, but I didn't dare stop or I'd never get going again.

At last, up across the hot sand to the base of the twisted cottonwoods, and there was my landing spot. I braced myself, tipped the pack slightly to the left, then kicked my feet loose as the load slammed me to the ground. For a long while I was content to just lie there, still strapped into the pack. Turning my head to the right, I could see my grub bag and stove hanging from the tree. Everything looked untouched.

Out of the pack and standing up, I was amazed at how light I felt on my feet — about two hundred pounds lighter. It was time to rattle them pots 'n' pans. Down came the stove and grub bag. Within minutes, a meal was in the making. While dinner was cooking I unloaded the pack and hung the meat high up in the cottonwood.

It was late afternoon by the time dinner and dishes were out of the way. Very few bugs had discovered me yet. I suppose the steady wind over the past week had blown them deep into the timber. For now, the breeze remained gentle as I set up the tent and rolled out my bed.

With all the chores done, I could light a good hot fire and heat up some rocks and water for a sweat lodge. Once the fire was going good and hot, I cut a half-dozen long willow poles and fashioned them into an igloo shape. Then I covered it in with a big tarp, throwing sand against the outside walls to hold everything down. I made a seat inside of an up-side-down pail covered with a towel. While the rocks were heating up, I sat back on the beach and enjoyed a cold beer. Gradually, all the hardships seemed barely to have happened.

When the rocks were ready, I began to take my boots off, but soon discovered why my feet were so sore. I was blistered from heel to toe and the skin stayed in my socks when I pulled them off. I carefully removed the rest of my clothes, then put on a clean pair of cotton tube socks and sneakers.

Next came the fun part. I filled four ice-cream pails with water that was just too hot for the skin and placed them inside the lodge. I placed a large tin pail of boiling water beside them. With my axe, I rolled two big hot rocks into the metal wash basin and placed it inside the lodge. Finally, I scooted into the lodge with my soap, shampoo, face cloth and a cup, and closed the flap.

The lodge was already hot in the sun, so when I started splashing boiling water on the rocks it got very interesting in a hurry. Before long, rivers of sweat were pouring out of my hair and down my sides. Time for a rinse. Out the door and into the milky blue glacial water I went.

Back inside, after a few more cups of boiling water were poured over the rocks, I shampooed my hair and rinsed with water from the ice-cream pails. By the time I was finished scrubbing up, I resembled a human again. Clean clothes suddenly felt cool and refreshing. To end the day, I relaxed by the fire and watched the sun go down. The next day was going to be a long one, so I turned in early with my sheep horns and cape by my side.

As the morning sun hit my tent, it seemed as if I had just fallen asleep. Since the plane wouldn't arrive until 1:00 PM, I had plenty of time to have breakfast, break camp and try the fishing. By midday, all the chores were done and my small pile of gear was waiting by the shore. It was time to try for a lake trout. On the very first cast I nailed one and soon had him hanging from a shaded willow. My second cast got the very same result.

Putting my rod away, I cleaned these two three-pound-beauties and rolled them up in a wet burlap sack to keep cool.

Soon, I picked up the familiar sound of the Beaver as he broke out of the narrow pass behind camp. I kept the sheep hidden until Cameron was standing out on the float.

"Well," he said, "did you find any rams?"

"Yep," I answered as I lifted the horns up from behind my gear.

Cameron's eyes popped open as he jumped onto the beach and grabbed them out of my hand. He was so happy, you'd think he'd gotten the ram himself. "Why are you so early?" I asked, looking at my watch.

"I couldn't wait to see how you made out," he said.

On the flight back to Dease Lake, I spotted a small lake below and asked Cameron, "Can you take off from that little lake down there?" He banked the plane way over, then back and said, "Sure, no problem."

"Good," I said, "I may go there for a moose someday."

This was one hell of an adventure. The valuable lessons I learned on this hunt would make my many future hunts much more enjoyable. I gave the two lake trout to a little kid at the "Jake Break" truck stop in Dease Lake. You would have thought I'd given him a new bicycle.

On arriving in Stewart, I discovered I had lost twenty pounds in nine days. Dr. Kuntz was happy about that, but he wasn't too thrilled when I woke up twice on the operating table.

•••

4

Dodd's First Moose...

To say that he was excited would have been a gross understatement. He was fairly vibrating. After missing out on our sheep hunt last year because of a crushed hand, he was more than ready for action.

Dodd was only eighteen at the time, but was an exceptional hunting partner. He was just learning to hunt, so he didn't have any bad habits, as yet. He was as strong as a bear, and was eager to learn. This meant that I had a chance to create the almost perfect hunting partner. What I really needed to do now was to find him a pack frame that would carry a four-hundred-pound load.

In preparation for the trip, I gave him a list of everything he would need to bring, including a warm sleeping bag. With our gear all packed, it was time to pick up our groceries We headed down to the grocery store and loaded up with everything on the 'not fit for human consumption' list. Then it was off to the liquor store for a magnum bottle of Lemon Hart cough medicine.

After a good night's sleep, we threw our gear into the back of my tired old Datsun pick-up and pointed her for Dease Lake. Along the way, on an old abandoned air strip we stopped for lunch, set up a target, and checked our rifles.

Dodd is left handed, so his very first rifle, of which he is extremely proud, was a .308 Savage. He was using 150-grain hand-loads, and placed his shots well. I was using 85-grain Nosler partitions in my .243, and found them a fairly deadly combination.

Arriving at Dease Lake, we headed for the BC-Yukon float base, and double-checked our flight schedule. We were still on for mid-morning, so we headed to the Bradford's, where we stayed the night.

Morning found us frowning back at the dark clouds. We could be in for a 'soaker' but we'd take it just the same. After coffee, we drove down to the float base and unloaded our gear. Shortly, we heard the familiar drone of the Beaver as he returned from his first trip of the day. The whole time Dodd was bombarding me with questions about the bush, our gear, the weather, moose, grizzlies, caribou, the Beaver float plane …

Finally, we were loaded, and on our way. Our destination was a small lake I'd spotted from the air while returning from last year's sheep hunt.

As we approached the lake, I spotted a black bear sow with two first year cubs running across a long narrow meadow. This was not a familiar sight in the northern high country. To grizzlies and wolves, the black bear is quite a tasty treat. Here close to the timberline, the scattered patches of spruce and balsam offered the bear and her cubs minimal protection.

After another near perfect BC-Yukon landing we scanned the eastern shore for a dry spot to unload our gear. A large mound resembling an old beaver house looked perfect.

The aircraft was gone within minutes, and there we sat in silence on our pile of gear. Now that we were on the ground, I was quite satisfied that this lake was a good choice. Three hundred yards across the lake, to the west, a fifty-yard buffer of stunted willow and arctic birch separated the lake from the low, sparsely-timbered ridge beyond. To the north and south ran wide grassy meadows broken intermittently by low wandering ridges clothed in flaming red arctic birch. To the east, about two hundred yards across a grassy willow bottom was a flat bench with fairly good-sized timber growing along it.

I turned to Dodd and said, "Let's just grab our rifles and go for a little stroll." Inside the timber's edge we found the perfect campsite. It was a natural opening in the balsam with a little creek running only thirty yards to the south.

By mid-afternoon, we had our camp all set up, and a big meal in our bellies. I was having a hard time holding Dodd down, so I said, "How about sitting out on the grass for a while, and see if we can get attacked by a moose?" He was wired. He didn't know what he wanted to do, but he wanted to do it right now!

About forty yards north of the camp was a grassy opening on the edge of the bench. We got comfortable out there, where we could see all of the west side and some of the south end of the lake. The sun was breaking through from time to time, so it was not too cold. The bugs were, thankfully, gone for another year. As we sat there, Dodd fidgeted around and came up with a million suggestions as to what we should be doing. All of them were the same: "Let's just go and find a moose!"

I was rescued from this lively interrogation by the arrival of Mrs Moose and her lovely calf. She had just stepped out of the timber across the lake, and was now feeding along slowly toward the north, her calf following close by her side. This old girl had obviously had a marvellous summer, as she was absolutely rolling in fat and appeared to be the size of the average boxcar.

As Dodd entertained himself watching the cow and her calf, I spotted a movement to the left. There, coming into the open on the cow's fresh tracks were two very gung-ho young bull moose. Quietly, I said, "Dodd, look back to the left."

He lowered his bino's and, as his eyes picked up the moose he nearly jumped out of his skin. "Bulls, Ferg, they're both bulls!" he hissed.

"Yep," I answered, "but they're just babies. We won't be shooting any babies in this country."

His eyes popped right out of his head. "But Ferg, there's our winter meat! One for you and one for me! We can shoot them from this side!"

He was frantic as I sat there watching the two bulls close in behind the cow. Suddenly, the cow turned, and with her ears laid back, glared at the bulls. They got the message and backed off. The whole time Dodd was glaring at me, wondering what he had to do before I'd let him shoot one of the young bulls.

"Relax Dodd" I said, "the big guys will start moving fairly soon."

"Fairly soon?" he said, "Fairly soon it's going to be dark!"

Just then, I spotted something out of place to the south. My bino's told me it was a huge swaying rack of a bull moose, materializing out of the timber beyond the end of the lake.

"Well Dodd," I said, "there's your moose!" He saw where I was looking and lifted his bino's. Now he became a tad more excited.

"He's going to cross that big meadow. We'll have to hurry if we're going to head him off" I said.

We grabbed our rifles and headed out on the run. We had over a half a mile to go, so we were really pouring it on. As we topped a low ridge, the bull was entering a narrow strip of timber on another ridge. If he kept on going he would cross an even wider meadow to the north. Then, I spotted another big bull breaking into the open from the same spot as the first. He wasn't as big, but was a mighty fine bull just the same. We carried on our race across an open grassy meadow and into the cover of a few scattered scrub willows. By this time, the big guy in the lead was breaking into the north meadow and moving slightly toward us. He was still about six hundred yards away, but now we could hear his grunts. The second bull was crossing the low timbered ridge. Every time the big guy lowered his head to rip up the brush, we moved ahead quickly. When he lifted his head, we would freeze. When he was half way across the meadow, the second one came out of the timber and launched into a major landscaping project. He had arctic birch and moss flying in every direction.

This only served to enrage the first bull, who started his own little project. He was only four hundred yards out, and for the first time we got a good look at his incredible antlers. They appeared to be over sixty inches across, with massive wide palms.

We had a problem. We needed to get much closer to attempt a shot under those conditions. A short, bushy spruce one hundred and fifty yards ahead, and out in the open would give us cover if we could get it lined up between us and the bull. He was moving slowly again. As his head disappeared behind the tree, we took off running toward him, and found better cover close to the timber on out left. We kept moving every chance we got, but he made the timber about two hundred yards in front of us. The second bull, still in the meadow, was re-landscaping the first bull's fine work.

We took advantage of this project to rush within range of the spot where the first bull had entered the timber. Then we discovered how the first bull had vanished so quickly. A low grassy ridge jutting out into the meadow covered his last fifty yards in the open.

As we crouched side by side on the edge of this little hump, facing the second bull, the first bull was less than forty yards to our left, just inside the timber. He had switched over to a logging project as he grunted and snorted, and played havoc in the timber. At this range, his terrific grunts and snorts were almost terrifying, as he waited to face his rival. Try as we may, we couldn't get a look at him.

The second bull was, by then, within forty yards, so I whispered to Dodd, "Let's take him in the neck, six inches behind the ear." Dodd gave me 'thumbs up'.

Our excitement level was up in the red as the bull closed to within thirty yards, still snorting violently and ripping up willows. Suddenly, quiet as a cat, he started up the slope. Then, as suddenly, he froze: he had spotted us. We were silhouetted against the lake in the background, but he couldn't tell just what we were.

Dodd and I both had our crosshairs on his neck, waiting for him to move. The instant he moved his head, I fired, and he swayed to the right, but stayed on his feet. I fed another round into the chamber and took a quick glance at Dodd. His mouth was hanging open, and his eyes were popping out.

"Come on, shoot!" I yelled, as I lined up and fired again. This time I heard his shot in unison with mine, and the big bull tipped over for good. Re-loading, we walked over to the bull. His neck was broken, but he was still snorting violently.

"Dodd, quick, put another one in his neck!", I said. At the shot, the big guy relaxed, and a strange hush fell over the land. The other bull had faded away into the timber, and there we stood in the twilight, grinning.

I reached out and shook Dodd's hand, "Good work, partner." I said, "Now we've got our winter meat!"

Fig 8:
"Good work, partner." I said, "Now we've got our winter meat!"

Our work was cut out for us, as the bull was lying on a steep slope with his hind end down in the willows. It could have been worse; he could have been lying in the water. With little time to waste we got down to work and field dressed him before it got too dark. By the time we were done, there was very little light left to help us get back to camp. A flashlight would have been a treat.

I stopped along the edge of the timber after a very interesting stroll in the dark.

"I think we're right close to camp here somewhere, Dodd. Stay here while I have a look."

Dodd said, "Well, we should be fairly close; we just crossed that little creek."

Fig 9:
Dodd heads for camp with the final load.

As I stumbled around in the darkness, I made out something that seemed out of place. I took a few careful steps and reached out my hand — it was our tent!

"We're home Dodd! Let's get a fire going and have a bite to eat."

"Right on!" he said, "I'm a little hungry now."

A friendly fire was burning within minutes, and we were enjoying a cup of tea with our bedtime snack.

Somewhere around daylight, I awoke to a strange vibrating, humming sort of a noise. Without moving, I opened my eyes, listening intently. It seemed to be coming from nearby. Then a particularly violent vibration caught my attention to my left. It was Dodd. He was shivering so hard the whole tent was shaking. And rightly so, our cheap little nylon wall tent was completely covered in frost- inside and out.

With particular dread, I unzipped my cozy down filled bag and slith- ered into my frozen, blood soaked clothes. Outside the tent, everything was frozen solid, including the water pail. After a quick trip to the creek I had water on for coffee. Then I lit a nice hot fire to take the kinks out while breakfast was cooking. After awhile, I coaxed Dodd out of bed.

I handed him a cup of coffee and said, "Good morning, you look like crap!"

He said "That's how I feel! You snored all night long! I turned my flashlight on and you were lying on your back with your sleeping bag wide open, sweating! And here I was curled up in this cheap cotton bag, freezing to death!"

At that point, I had to laugh, because we had gotten into quite a lively discussion about the quality of his sleeping bag before leaving Stewart.

We checked over our gear after a big breakfast, to make sure we had all the weapons we'd need to cut up our bull. Dodd took his .308, in the event of an argument over the moose when we got there, and away we went. Thankfully, nothing was on the kill to greet us. The sun had just come up, making for a good photo session.

We got down to work, skinning and struggling, as we tried to keep the meat clean. Hard work and persistence paid off when all the meat was finally up on the grass ready to load up. After a few more photos, we loaded our pack frames and headed for the grassy hump by the shore. It was less than half a mile, so things moved along quite nicely. By mid afternoon, all the meat was stacked up at the lake and we were up in camp having a dishpan bath.

With clean clothes and sneakers on, sipping cocktails, and cooking fillet for dinner, we felt quite smug. As most moose hunters know, fillet of moose is pretty hard to beat. After dinner, we retired to the campfire and launched into a lively marathon of laughs and lies. By the time we hit the sack, we were in no danger of waking up during the night, as we had severely wounded our bottle of cough medicine.

The next three days were most enjoyable. We half-heartedly hunted caribou, but for the most part, we simply relaxed around camp and ate lots of moose meat. Dodd and I would go on many more hunts together. Sometimes we would come home with game and other times not. It didn't matter; we always had more fun than we could handle.

•••

5

Moose and Caribou Hunt With the Good Ol' Boys...

In early October of 1981, I made my annual pilgrimage, a gruelling eighteen-hour drive in my beat-up old Datsun pick-up, from Stewart, BC to the Douglas Lake Ranch. This great sprawling rangeland had been my home for the first twenty years of my life.

The early years saw me in the one-room school at the home ranch, gazing out the windows at the surrounding hillsides. I felt much akin to a wolf in a cage until September, when grouse season opened. This was the day I waited all year for. I was up before daylight cooking up a big breakfast of bacon, eggs, fried potatoes and toast on our old wood stove. Then I would throw a crude peanut butter and jam sandwich together, toss it in a bag, and I was ready to go. Shortly after daylight, I would be riding down the road on my rickety old bicycle with my 16 gauge single shot Cooey slung across my back with bailer twine. "Stand back, boys — here comes that wild Ferguson kid!"

I would show up at home after dark tired, hungry, and happy with my basket full of grouse and a three-chapter story to tell about how I got each and every one of them. Of course the grouse season was merely a warm-up to the duck and goose season two weeks later. Although it was always fun to get the odd goose, I was more of a duck hunter. I found it better to wait until after thanksgiving before shooting any waterfowl. This way all of the pinfeathers had fully developed and the ducks were nearly too fat to fly. We ate duck at least once a week all through the season, right up until Christmas.

On this particular trip, I wanted to get enough birds for a few good feeds for my family and friends. I also hoped to get a Christmas goose for my good friend Albert Claridge who was allergic to turkey.

A few weeks earlier, I had talked to my dad on the phone and he had asked me if I was going to make it down for the annual Thanksgiving weekend hunt with him, Chunky and their friends. (Chunky Woodward was the owner of the ranch and dad was the cow boss.)

At 5:00 PM on the first day of the hunt, I pulled up in front of the "big house" just in time to grab my old Ithaca pump and jump into one of Chunkie's Suburbans. Not until we drove twelve miles in two vehicles, set out the decoys and settled in to wait for the geese to show, did we have time to visit.

Fig 10:
Mike Ferguson and Charles "Chunky" Woodward.

Chunky's two sons John and Kip were there along with Tom Hinton, of BC Lions fame, and, at the time, on staff with MacMillan-Bloedel. I also met, for the first time, George Reiffele, Western Canadian director of Ducks Unlimited.

We had a great shoot that morning over the decoys. Then, after the birds quit flying, we concentrated our efforts on jump shooting potholes. By mid-afternoon we were all 'ducked out' so we headed for the shack. It was Miller time. Over our refreshments, I pulled out the little photo album of my most recent fly-in hunts. Chunky eagerly pored over the pictures of moose, caribou and sheep, and then turned to my dad and said, "Mike, we should go on one of these fly-in hunts with Pat before we get too old!" Tom didn't say much — his big grin just got bigger as I explained how I could set up the hunt.

They had all winter to think about it, and by July of '82 we had everything arranged. Dad and Peter Pulos, of Ye Old Spaghetti Factory fame, would drive to Stewart, pick me up, and we would drive to Dease Lake. The next morning, we would load our gear into the BC-Yukon Air Services Beaver for the flight to our chosen lake. In the meantime, Chunky and the other three hunters would fly from Vancouver to Watson Lake in Chunky's Cessna Citation. There they would board BC-Yukon's Otter for the flight into the same lake. We had it all arranged so that we would arrive at the lake two hours before they did. That way, we would have all the tents and the kitchen set up.

Fig 11:
Mike Ferguson arrives at "Camp Havoc."

September finally showed up and everything went like clockwork. Ray Sande and his crew did a fine job of getting us in there safe and on time. The weather was picture-perfect with a massive high-pressure system holding firmly over northern BC and the Yukon.

We had just set up the tents when we heard the familiar sound of the Otter as it cruised into sight around a mountain to the north. There is something about the sound of an Otter that gives me goose bumps, and I like it. He circled our camp at the southeast corner of the lake to check for rocks in the water, then flew to the north end to start his approach.

As usual, Ray put the old girl on the water like nobody can, and was soon drifting quietly into shore. When he opened up the freight door, three of the most ornery looking critters I ever had the misfortune to meet stepped down onto the pontoon. It was Tom Hinton, all 260 pounds of him, his little brother Joe at 240 pounds, and their brother-in-law Dr. Jerry Johnston. Joe, in the past, had tried out for the BC Lions and was at this time a college dean in Texas. 'Doc' had a seven-chair dental practice in Ruston, Louisiana. He was also a fitness lunatic, jogging ten miles every day before going to work and it showed. He was of medium height, but his legs were like tree trunks.

The last man out of the Otter was Chunky in his black cowboy hat. The miles of rolling tundra must have reminded Chunky of the ranch. He stepped ashore with that sparkling Woodward smile on his face and said to my dad, "Damn, Mike! Can you imagine how many cattle we could run up here?"

The ol' man laughed and said, "Oh, sure! It would work just fine until they all starved to death!"

We all took an armful of gear and headed up the hill toward camp, which was at the top of a low ridge in a loose patch of twisted balsam. Tom introduced me to Joe and Doc as we headed back down for another load.

Meanwhile, Ray had taxied up the lake to the north and was just beginning his take-off run. The old beast charged onto the step with a throaty roar and was in the air in seconds. Everyone had their cameras out as Ray thundered by in his 'baby', dipping the wing as he passed.

Soon the high valley was quiet again. Even our voices seemed to be dampened by the tundra as we went about the business of settling in.

When we brought the coolers up, I could see that this was going to be a hunt like no other I had been on. Chunky liked to do the cooking on all of his hunts, which suited me just fine, but I wasn't prepared for what I saw when he opened up the coolers. There was a complete meal prepared for each day of the hunt complete with trimmings and desserts. There was also a big box full of painkillers in colours ranging from clear to dark amber.

My first suggestion, that we not light a big fire and make a lot of noise, went over like a Sadam Hussein tour of Texas so I quickly let it drop.

It was mid-afternoon and beginning to cool off, so I got out my spotting scope and tripod to have a little squint around. I wasn't long in spotting caribou on the mountaintop across the south end of the lake. A bull and several cows fed from behind a ridge. He was a good two miles away, and I couldn't tell how big he was, except that he was wearing all of his beautiful fall colours. The flowing white mane of a mature caribou bull in mid-to-late September is a sight to behold. They moved out of sight behind another ridge before I had a chance to show anyone, leaving everyone thinking, "Just how full of that which flows out of the south end of a northbound male caribou is this guy?" Well, it was all mind over matter: I didn't mind so it didn't matter.

We poured ourselves cocktails and launched into a lively visit while Chunky and Peter got dinner warmed up. The first night was rough. We were forced to suffer through a game stew made up of venison, goose, duck, grouse, pheasant and other unidentified but incredibly delicious morsels. For dessert, we had cherry cheesecake with coffee and liqueur. I felt the faintest little twinge of guilt as I thought about my lovely wife Ida, sitting at home with our three kids, worrying her little heart about me and the terrible hardships here in the hostile frozen north. I wasn't long in getting that thought out of my head as the fire got taller and the talk got louder. It seemed I was destined to have a good time whether I wanted to or not.

Morning arrived, clear and cold. When I crawled out of my tent at daylight, Dad and Chunky were already standing by the fire drinking coffee. I poured myself a black one and joined the conversation. Doc was the next one out of the sack, dressed in his down-filled jumpsuit. He didn't say a word as we walked over to the kitchen and grabbed a cup, poured himself a shot and came to the fire. He stared into the flames for a few seconds then moved closer to me and, in his very best southern accent, said: "Now Pat, y'all find me a moose today. Ah'm fixin' ta kill his ass!" That ripped it! I burst out laughing and nearly fell into the fire!

Before long Chunky had his big griddle hot on the three-burner propane stove with bacon, eggs and pancakes on the way. With a hot breakfast in our bellies, we were soon ready to go. Dad and Chunky decided to go up the mountain to the northwest where I had seen the bull and cows. Tom, Joe and Doc wanted to go over the ridge behind camp. Peter opted to stay and hunt close to camp. I took out the little piece of map I had laminated and pointed out where I was going to go. I wanted to circle the mountain that Dad and Chunky were going up.

We wished each other good luck and were all heading out of camp by the time the sun touched the peaks. For the first three miles, I didn't stop for long to glass, as it was still very cold. There was caribou sign at every step, but I didn't see a single animal all morning. By midday, the air was quite warm. I made my way around to a prominent point on the extreme northwest corner of the mountain. According to my map, a broad basin nestled in the north-facing slope of the mountain, and I wanted to stop and rest where I could glass it for awhile.

As I rounded the shoulder of the mountain, the basin came into sight, over two miles wide and three miles from the top to the scattered balsams below. I found a sunny spot out of the wind and settled in. Using my bino's, I spotted caribou immediately, and lots of them. I moved to the spotting scope and began checking over the bulls. Out of fifty-six caribou, I could see only one big bull, and he wasn't what most hunters would consider a trophy. But he was hog fat. Since they were all beginning to bed down for the day, with the sun finally reaching into the basin, I didn't have to be in a hurry to make a move.

Fig 12:
"Camp was on a low ridge at the south end of the lake."

I got out a bag of trail mix and my water jug and snacked as I continued to scan the bottom of the basin. A flash of white caught my eye and I focussed my scope on it. A big bull moose materialized out of the balsams, sporting at least a fifty-five inch set of antlers. He was the ultimate picture of health; as he walked his impressive rack swayed slowly from side to side. He was obviously doing an antler display for another moose somewhere in the nearby timber.

Beyond the thin strip of timber below lay a flat, marshy valley four miles wide and over twenty miles long. Through the spotting scope, I could make out little groups of caribou as they relaxed, each in the company of a head bull. In another week the rut would be in full swing, and the meat would change from delicious to putrid.

Although the sun was bright and the sky clear, it was still chilly at the six thousand foot level. I decided to move down into the basin and get a mile or so closer to the herd. This I accomplished without being spotted and was soon sitting on the sunny side of a twenty-foot wide bowl on the mountainside. I was about a half-mile from the herd, but the bull I wanted was bedded on the far side. There was plenty of time, so I decided to let him make the first move.

64

Munching a granola bar, I studied the different animals in the herd. One young bull in particular grabbed my attention. His face and neck were a dark chocolate brown and his bloody antlers had torn strips of velvet hanging from them. He had evidently begun shedding his velvet during the night and was in a quandary as to how to utilize all this testosterone. The females of the herd, much to his frustration, simply ignored him as he ran around snorting, shaking his antlers and rearing up on his hind legs like a stallion.

A lone cow near the timber at the lower end of the herd appeared to be sick or injured. She stood for some time with her head hanging and a hump in her back. Then she would lie down for a few minutes and immediately get up again. She was standing on a bench thirty feet above a small creek that issued from a spring below and to my left. The bright sun was making me drowsy, so I found a comfortable position in the tundra, pulled my cap over my eyes and dozed off.

"Whoof! Snort!"

"**W**hat the hell?" I said as I sat up rubbing my eyes. Did I hear something or was I having a dream? As my eyes came back into focus I noticed a broad patch of torn up tundra lying with its roots up, ten feet away. I stood up and took a quick look around, thinking at first that Dad and Chunky had pulled a sneak on me. The only place close to me that I couldn't see was behind the swell of the hill directly below. I stepped out on the edge of the bowl and got the shock of my life as a big silvertip grizzly burst out onto the flats. He was charging down the creek bed, his fall coat flashing in the sun with every jump. He looked back at me over his right shoulder as if to say, "Don't shoot!"

It then became clear that he was headed straight down the creek toward the sick cow. The noise he was creating had attracted her attention from a half-mile away. As he closed in on her she sank slowly to the ground, and watched him rush by her at spitting distance. After he had vanished into the timber, she stood up and carried on with her illness. It was only then that I began to consider the situation that I had been in and how the whole show might have looked from across the basin through the spotting scope.

Here is the hunter, snoozing the afternoon away in his fluffy bed of tundra without a care in the world. Meanwhile, here comes a big boar grizzly snooping his way up the mountain unaware of the man with the rifle when he bumps into a pair of hiking boots with his nose. Exit downhill, with after burners fully engaged.

Thank God, I had put my cap over my face. There are some things easier to live through if you just don't participate.

Fig 13:
"Some things are easier to live through if you just don't participate."

By this time, some of the herd were on their feet feeding, so I began to make my move. I threaded my way down along the creek to where a small tributary joined it. I followed it for four or five hundred yards until I reached a prominent hump. So far, none of the caribou had spotted me, but the big bull was still four hundred yards away and lying down. This gave me time to settle down and find a good rest. After nestling in behind the .243, I noted a few stems of grass sticking up in the line of fire, so I crawled out and removed them. Back into position again, everything looked perfect. I noticed with some anxiety that it was already late afternoon and I was still four miles from camp.

As if he had read my mind, he casually stood up and had a good stretch. He was clear of the others, so holding about two feet over the top of his back, I squeezed off the shot and watched for the impact. He took two quick steps forward and stood with his head slightly lowered. He didn't move a hair for about twenty seconds, then just tipped over and fell stiff legged on his left side — a perfect lung shot.

The young bull with the bloody antlers seized the moment and went into his tough-guy routine again as he spotted me getting out my camera gear. I stayed partly hidden, so that he couldn't identify me, and it worked. He came trotting across the mountainside above me snorting and puffing, his eyes popped out like big black marbles. I took some good footage of him on my super-8 movie camera as he reared up on his hind legs and raced away, only to turn around and trot right back again, toes clicking together all the way. While he was still in close, I located my Canon AE-1 with Vivitar 70-210 telephoto lens and snapped a few photos.

With time running out, I gathered my gear and hiked across the tundra to my bull. He was a little past his prime, but still in good health and he didn't smell at all like a bull in the rut. Had I shot this same bull two weeks later the smell would likely have gagged a maggot.

I set up the camera on the tripod and took a few photos, then got down to the knife work. I was sure it was going to freeze hard again overnight, so I didn't cut him up. I just gutted him and cut his flanks out so the body cavity would cool quickly.

Once the liver, heart, kidneys, tongue and fillets were in my pack, I marked my territory around the bull and headed for camp. By the time I had made it up through the pass, the light was fading fast. I could see our camp over two miles below with a friendly fire burning. As I made my way carefully down the mountainside, I tried to guess what Chunky had cooked up for us this time. My stomach began to growl, so I tried to think about something else.

About the time it got real good and dark, I did find something to think about — that damn grizzly! I knew the old man would be worrying quietly to himself about me, so, part way down the mountainside, I let out a cowboy whoop. In just a few seconds Dad answered with a whoop of his own. Peter, bless his heart, jumped into the zodiac and rowed across the lake to pick me up, saving me a long walk.

When I reached the shore, Peter was full of good news, and, as we crossed the lake, he let me have it. Everyone had gotten back to camp early. Dad and Chunky had bagged a caribou and he had one as well. They had been standing around the fire celebrating and enjoying a cocktail when someone said "Moose!" A big bull with about fifty-three inch wide antlers had walked right out onto the flat at the end of the lake. Four guys scrambled for their rifles and ran to the crest of the ridge sliding to a stop on their bellies. Within seconds, the bull had surrendered and the whole camp was on its way down to check out a thousand pounds of steaks and roasts.

Fig 14:
"He was a little past his prime, but still in good health..."

Needless to say, there was an air of excitement about as Peter and I trudged up the hill toward camp. As I approached the fire, I was met by a circle of grinning faces. Chunky handed me a glass of scotch and, before I had a chance to say anything, Joe took the floor. He started out with: "Now lookit! Y'all told us not ta' light a far and don't make any noise 'round the camp an' what-all! Well it took a bunch o' good ol' boys from the South ta' show y'all how ta' hunt moose! First ya gotta get ya some real drinkin' whisky an' get somma that in ya! Then ya gotta talk real loud and laugh real hard! That's the way ta' hunt moose!"

All the way through Joe's speech we roared and laughed. He was, without a doubt, the wildest man I had met in a day or two and kept us entertained for the entire trip. He was also the only one in camp that could even come close to out-snoring the old man.

They all wanted to hear what I had done all day, so I got after it. When I reached the part about the grizzly, I had their undivided attention. Before long, I had lots of help to pack my caribou back to camp, as Tom had a grizzly tag. I dished up my meal, which happened to be lasagne, and sat down near the fire to enjoy it.

Morning found me heading back up the mountain with Tom, Doc and Peter in tow. On the north side of the pass we sat down and glassed the whole basin, but spotted nothing. We cut up the bull and I loaded Tom and Peter up and sent them on their way. Doc and I cut the rest of it up, chopped out the antlers, and loaded our packs. When we started out, we could still see Tom and Peter as they made their way up into the pass half a mile away.

Suddenly, I noticed movement down the slope from them. It was a herd of sixteen caribou running up the hill, and they were watching Tom and Peter. Doc and I got down on our bellies right where we were on a little hump. The herd stopped and stared at them for a while, then turned and ran straight up at us from about six hundred yards. With the antlers on top of my pack, they thought I was a bedded caribou.

At sixty yards the caribou stopped and turned broadside to look back at them again. By this time Doc was about to have a fit and blurted out, "Gawd damn! I ain't never shot me a caribou before!" I was having so much fun watching the show, I forgot that we were still hunting!

"Okay, Doc," I said, "take that bull on the right with the white mane."

He wiggled out of his pack and crawled into position behind his .300 Weatherby Magnum. At the shot the only thing that happened was muzzle blast. "Doc!" I said, "crawl ahead a little farther! Your bullet exploded in the grass!" Meanwhile the herd was milling around in confusion at the clap of thunder, giving Doc a chance to get lined up again. At the second shot, the bull dropped as if hit by lightning. Then, just as quickly, he jumped to his feet, ran in a tight circle and tipped over.

I reached out and slapped Doc on the side of the leg and said, "Good work, Doc, more meat for my freezer!" Tom and Peter had stood watching the whole performance, and instead of offering to take a bigger load, turned away and headed over the pass Perhaps they felt that their one hundred pound loads were plenty for this trip.

As the rest of the herd ran off, Doc and I took a few photos and got to work cutting up his bull. We loaded what meat we could into our already heavy packs, stacked the rest up to cool on a rock pile, and headed for camp.

When Tom and Peter came into sight of camp they sat down for a breather and a little look around. Tom trained his bino's on camp and said, "Y'all see that tent down there?"

Peter, with a confused look on his face, said, "I surely do see that tent down there."

"In that tent," Tom carried on, "is a duffle bag, and in that bag is a bottle o' drinkin' whisky! When I get to camp I'm gonna get me somma' that whisky. Then I'm gonna walk over and take hold of ol' Mike and whup his ass for raisin' that S.O.B.!"

Doc and I were the last to arrive in camp that day, and, by the time we got there, it was clear that Tom had already gotten into the duffle bag. I had no sooner shed my heavy load when Tom had me by both shoulders and hoisted me clear off the ground. With a big grin on his face and roaring laughter in the background, he said, "Now y'all knew that ol' grizzly bear wasn't gonna be there today, didn't ya? Y'all just wanted a few pack horses to carry your meat back to camp, didn't ya?" What could I say? With no traction and his big meat hooks clamped onto me, all I could do was laugh.

He finally set me back on the ground and helped me hang the meat up to cool. That night we enjoyed another of Chunky's famous meals before retiring to the fire for another round of 'bedtime stories'.

The next morning was clear and cold again, promising a typical bugless mid-September day. Tom, Joe and Doc had decided to take a tour out to the east again. Dad, Chunky and Peter were still not sure what they wanted to do, but I had one more big load of meat to pack in. I wasted little time in getting started.

By the time I had crossed the end of the lake to the sunny side and made my way up through the thin strip of balsam timber, I was already in a sweat and the sun was really cranking up the heat. At the last patch of balsam, I was suddenly struck by a wave of genius. I thought, "if I get naked I bet I can make real good time going up this mountain!"

I got out of my boots, pulled off my heavy wool pants and long underwear, then pulled my boots back on. I was right! I could take longer steps and more of them without heating up. I was practically flying up the mountain when I glanced across the lake at the abandoned outfitters' camp. There was something different about it this particular day; it wasn't abandoned. In fact, there were three or four people out in the open with bino's very intently studying the mountainside I was on. I paused briefly for a breather and had a look at them through my bino's. Now two more people joined the fun, one with a spotting scope and tripod. I still had half a mile to go, but for some reason I made it over the top in record time.

I spent most of the day taking pictures and snoozing in the sun. By mid-afternoon the air was beginning to cool off, so I loaded up the rest of Doc's caribou and headed for camp. It was a brutal load, but the thought of a full freezer kept me upbeat all the way.

When I arrived in camp, Dad, Chunky and Peter were sitting around the fire visiting over a cocktail as our supper warmed up. They all helped me out of my pack, then Peter asked, "What the heck were you wearing on your way up the mountain this morning?"

I laughed. "What did it look like?" I asked.

"I don't know!" he answered. "I've never seen anything flash so bright in the sun before! Was that your long-john's?"

"Naw," I said, "that was my birthday suit!"

Tom, Joe and Doc were the last ones into camp that evening with a big load of moose meat and an even bigger moose-hunting story. The longer we sat around the fire that night, the bigger and more vicious the bull became. By the time we headed off the bed, he was the new world-record Canada moose.

The next morning, the Hinton Gang went back to get the rest of their bull and the antlers while Peter and I went out to the end of a ridge south of camp to have a look around. The valley below was five miles wide and nearly twenty miles long with hardly a tree in it! It didn't take us long to spot a moose. About three miles away a big bull, with antlers over sixty inches wide, was guarding a cow from a smaller bull of about fifty-five inches. He would walk slowly toward the younger bull with his huge rack swaying from side to side then, from about fifty feet, he would suddenly rush in and try to hook him. The young bull would escape the dangerous antler tips every time, only to circle back for another try. We watched this performance until they all came to their senses and bedded down for the rest of the day. There were no bugs left and very little wind to bother us, so we snoozed away the rest of the afternoon in peace and quiet.

That night the Hinton crew staggered into camp with a truckload of meat and a 56-inch-wide set of moose antlers. Joe had come to the conclusion that he was as physically fit as any man could possibly be, so he decided to stay in camp and relax the next day. Tom and Doc, on the other hand, were not quite in his condition, so they planned a two-day tour for stone sheep. That night, they got their gear sorted out, including my little dome tent and cook stove. Tom, Doc and I studied the map under the flashlight and came up with a rough plan of attack for the morning.

Shortly after daylight, we were enjoying another of Chunky's hearty breakfasts. With their bellies full of pancakes, sausages and eggs, Tom and Doc headed out. The rest of us did a little fishing for arctic grayling and lake trout, but spent most of the day relaxing. Late in the afternoon, Jim and Lucy Wood flew over in their Cessna on a hunt of their own. They spotted us walking around camp and stopped in for a visit. Jim and

Chunky had met many years before in the Armed Forces, and were both happy to see each other once more.

That night, several miles east of base camp, Tom and Doc set up the little dome tent near the top of a rugged hog back. They hiked up to the top of the ridge and glassed the next basin for sheep until darkness closed in, then they had a bite to eat and went to bed.

Tom was having a wonderful sleep when Doc, who seemed to be fumbling with something in the darkness, accidentally nudged him awake. "What y'all doin' Doc?" He whispered.

"Damn, Tom," he whispered, "there's somethin' out there!"

"Go on back to sleep, Doc, there's nothin' out there. That's just the wind."

"I'm tellin' you, Tom, I heard somethin' sniffin' and lickin' at the tent!"

They both lay there listening for a time until Tom sat up and said, "Damn it, Doc, you're right! There is somethin' out there!"

Tom turned on his flashlight and pointed it at the side of the tent just in time to see the shape of a nose pull back from the nylon directly above his pack frame. By this time, Doc had his Weatherby ready for action with the barrel across Tom's sleeping bag. As if on cue, the nose pushed back against the tent and Doc pushed back with the rifle barrel.

"I'm tellin' you Tom, whatever it is, I'm goin' to give him another nostril!"

"Damn , Doc, don't shoot that thang in here. You'll blow Fergie's tent up and he'll kill our sorry asses!"

They finally figured that there was more than one critter outside, so they unzipped the door and tried to spot them. It was useless, though; the visitors scurried away every time they moved around inside the tent. Tom eventually guessed rightly that the neighbours were a bunch of wolf pups trying to lick the caribou blood off his pack through the side of the tent. They went back to sleep and let the wolves play.

The next evening as the sun went down, Tom and Doc returned to base camp sheepless and sleepless. They kept us laughing long into the night as the story got better each time it was told.

On our last day in camp, we all relaxed and enjoyed ourselves. I set up my sweat lodge and cleaned up for the trip out in the morning, while some of the guys had sponge baths. The setting sun that evening cast a golden glow over the land. Seeing it gather, we decided to set up a photo shoot. Everyone picked up a set of antlers and posed for the camera. Since Joe had the biggest set of moose antlers in hand, he thought it fitting to impress his dominance on the rest of us by goring someone. As he searched the group for a likely victim, he briefly took his eyes off Big

Brother. This gave Tom a chance to arm himself with the other set of moose antlers and the wreck was on. Off to one side, Dad and Peter sparred with the caribou antlers, trying at the same time to avoid being run over by Tom and Joe. Doc and Chunky seized the opportunity to move somewhere safe.

Fig 15:
"As he searched the group for a likely victim, he briefly took his eyes off Big Brother. "

The sheep hunt had apparently brought Tom to the peak of conditioning for, although his antlers were much smaller than Joe's, Tom tumbled and dragged him back and forth through camp for twenty minutes. Joe claimed to have been brutally wounded in the battle, and it took a river of painkiller to see him safely to bed.

We had such a good time on this hunt that we planned another one for the next year. We went on that hunt and although we didn't bag a single animal, we had another fantastic time together.

Dad and Chunky have both passed on now, but they lived their lives right, taking hold of each day as if it was their last. Their ashes are scattered a few hundred yards apart on a hill overlooking the Douglas Lake Home Ranch. If you listen closely on the right kind of evening, you can still hear their laughter.

•••

6
Ida Bags a Pachyderm...

The principal and teachers of the Stewart Elementary School were not impressed. The very day after registering our daughter, Debbie, and our two sons, Mike and Chuckie, we pulled them out of school.

Problems at the school? Not at all. It was moose season and the Ferguson kids were finally old enough to help Ida and me pack in our winter meat supply. Debbie was ten, Mike, eight, and Chuckie, six. They'd been waiting all summer for this trip to begin, and there we were, headed north.

My hunting partner, Dodd Hareuther and his wife, Trudy, would also be with us on the trip. We chose to hunt a very remote and seldom hunted, square-shaped lake at the base of what appeared to be a good caribou mountain. Ideally, to feed both families, one caribou and a single big moose would be perfect, but we would be happy to take what we could get.

The trip to Dease Lake was interrupted by frequent blueberry picking forays. This gave the kids a chance to run around and burn off a little steam, and Dodd and me, a chance to glass the surrounding mountains.

After a dry, dusty five hour chuck wagon ride up the Stewart-Cassiar Highway, we arrived at Dease Lake. Our kids were soon off with the Bradford kids, Rebecca, Leland, and Devlin. Ida and Trudy visited with Sherry, while Dodd and I walked over to check with BC-Yukon Airways. The news was good. We were still on schedule and the weather was holding quite well.

Morning found us with our gear heaped up on the dock. Ida and I and the kids would go in on the first flight and set up camp, while the Beaver returned to pick up Dodd and Trudy and the rest of the gear. The trip went fairly well, except for Mike, who landed at the lake with his breakfast in a bag. The poor kid had obviously inherited my weak stomach.

From the air, we picked our campsite, the only spot on the lake where the timber came close to the water- the south side. Soon after landing, we had our gear piled on the shore, and the Beaver was on its way back to pick up Dodd and Trudy.

We found a cache in the timber, and near it, an old outfitter's campsite. We all grabbed an armful of gear from the shore and hiked up to the timber's edge, sixty yards away. A high plywood table had been nailed down to four balsam stakes in the middle of a cleared area. This would serve as our kitchen. Several long poles were standing against the cache, so we soon had a rough framework set up to stretch a large tarp over.

On our way down to the water to pick up some more gear, someone said "Dad! There's a caribou!" Sure enough, across a shallow bay to the East, a young bull made his lonely way northward. A quick look with the bino's told me he was not legal yet, with only four points on top, but that next year he would likely be a beauty. I set up the spotting scope on the tripod, so the kids could have a good look at him as he strode through the stunted willow and arctic birch.

When the bull was gone, we packed the last of our gear up the soggy slope to camp. Our tarp was 18' x 20', so there was room under it for a large dome tent for the kids, and a small one for Ida and me.

By the time we had our tents set up, the Beaver was back. We all went down to the lake and helped unload the plane. In minutes, the last load was in the grass and the Beaver was on its way back to Dease. We all stood by the shore and watched as he disappeared over the low ridge to the east. Soon, it was quiet again, with only the sound of light waves lapping against the shore.

We each grabbed a box of grub and headed for the kitchen. While Ida and I set up the kitchen and Dodd set up his tent, Trudy and the kids packed the last of the gear into camp. As soon as I found the ice cream pails, I gave them to Mike and Chuck to fill up. Debbie then got to work in her tent, rolling out all the mattresses and sleeping bags. Dodd and Trudy soon had their tent all set up and their beds made. By then Ida had a few snacks out to keep us happy until supper time.

We were all set up in less than two hours, so we could relax and let the rest of the trip unfold on its own. Shortly after eating, the two-kid demolition crew was ready for more action.

"Grab your Swede saws boys." I said as I headed up a trail, axe in hand, into the balsam. Before long we found a thick patch of good-sized balsam, about eight inches at the base and twenty feet high. I handed Mike the axe and walked back down to camp.

By the end of the day, we had glassed every inch of the north side of the lake. The only place for a moose to hide was a thin strip of timber a half mile beyond the far shore. Along the mile long eastern shore the stunted timber started two hundred yards up from the shore, then faded gradually into tundra within four hundred yards. To the west, where the lake ran out, the land fell away into a heavily timbered valley twelve miles wide. In the morning I intended to hunt the mountain south of camp, if for no better reason than to get a better look at this incredible land.

It was morning and we were raring to go. Over coffee, we spotted a big bull with about a fifty seven inch spread. He was courting a cow in the thin strip of timber across the lake.

As we ate breakfast, I asked Dodd, "Well, what do you want to do?"

He said, "I don't know. What do you want to do?"

I said, "I think I'm going to take Ida and the kids and go find a caribou on the mountain behind us."

He thought for a while. "Well," he said, "I think Trudy and I will just stay here and keep an eye on this bull for a while."

"OK, good enough." I answered.

We got the breakfast dishes out of the way and were soon ready to go. I shook Dodd's hand, "Good luck partner. Bring that big guy home tonight."

He grinned, "Never mind; you bring one home!"

I turned and headed out of camp to the east with Ida and the kids in tow. A wide grassy willow bottom started at the lakeshore near camp, and ran southeast all the way up to the timberline. The going was easy and we made good time. I thought walking directly into the rising sun, that things could be a lot worse. We could have been sitting in camp waiting for the rain to quit.

Right at the timberline, we topped out onto a most beautiful sight. It appeared to be a floating meadow surrounded by scattered patches of heather, dwarf balsam, arctic birch, willow and lichen-covered rocks. I stepped carefully onto the grassy carpet. The water came part way up my rubber boots, but I was still on top. I started across with Mike right behind me. His boots were shorter, but he was still all right. Soon we were all across the forty yards of Jell-O and standing on the tundra. We saved a long walk around by crossing there but Ida still had a wild look on her face. I made a note to be careful — she carries her own rifle these days.

We were on a wide, gently sloping bench that appeared to run around the mountain toward the West. As we followed this bench, we came upon fresh caribou tracks. A small herd, six or eight had recently come from the direction we were going. Soon we topped out on to another bench. This time, instead of grass, it was covered in mountain blueberries. The little bushes grew right along the ground, and were loaded with tiny, sweet berries. The kids dropped everything and ripped into the patch like three grizzly cubs. While they loaded up on fruit, I set up the spotting scope and checked on the big bull across the lake. He was back in the timber a little farther, but his huge white palms gave him away as they flashed white in the sun. I scanned the west end of the lake for Dodd, but didn't see him.

As the temperature rose, the black flies began to crawl out of the moss where they had been driven by the night-time frost. This time of year they were much like drunken drivers as they crash landed in your ear or up your nose. With hardly a breath of wind to keep them occupied, they convinced us to move to another bench higher up. We soon discovered another interesting spot as we headed across the blueberry bench. This time it was a small, deep pool about sixty feet across, surrounded by two foot high arctic birch. The mud around the edge was torn up with huge moose tracks. When the flies get bad, it's not uncommon to see one or more big bull moose lying partly submerged in a pool like this.

When we began our climb to the edge of the high bench, three hundred yards above, Chuckie suddenly became rich. He had found a shed caribou antler. This was quite an event for a kid who's pockets normally concealed only dead frogs, birds and sticklebacks.

"Dad!" he asked, "Can I keep this horn?"

"Chuckie" I answered, "don't waste your energy packing that thing all over the mountain. We'll have some nice new antlers for you to carry pretty soon."

Well, that ripped it. Now he had the meanest dad in the whole world. He stubbornly dragged the antler up hill for a while, until eventually, he spotted something even better: a bigger caribou antler. He quickly jettisoned his old antler and scrambled for the new one. Longer points, bigger bez, deeper shovel and heavier beams. There was no more any self-respecting collecto-maniac could want. Debbie was quite content with the tiny little cow antler she had picked up. Mike on the other hand, was keeping his eyes peeled for fresh moving antlers. He was the guy who followed directly behind the 'Bwana', with the spotting scope and tripod in hand.

On a prominent point, near the southwest corner of the mountain, we stopped for a rest. We were by then about two miles from camp. A good rule to follow is: 'Don't hunt moose any farther from camp than you want to carry one.'

Since we had a commanding view of most of the country between there and camp, we decided to relax and glass for a while. The only sound was the irritating drone of the black flies as they shot erratically around our faces. The fat copper coloured models in particular seem to be most prevalent this time of year.

After a while, Chuck broke the long silence. "Dad," he said, "when I grow up, I'm gonna' hire the Beaver and I'm gonna' come up here and pick up all these caribou horns."

We all had a good chuckle as Ida gave him a hug. I had to admit, he was certainly a determined little guy.

Something dark caught my eye. "Moose!" I exclaimed, as I grabbed for the binoc's.

I couldn't believe my eyes. He was about six hundred yards below us, moving slowly toward the little pool to our right. We picked up our gear and rushed along the bench to try to intercept him. We managed to stay out of sight most of the way. Soon, we were sitting on the bench three hundred yards directly above the pool. The bull was nearly there, but we didn't know if he was going to stop or not. We had to make a move.

To our right, was a shallow gully we could use. It ran down to the eastern end of the pool. I hurriedly instructed the kids to stay and watch, while Mom and I pulled a sneak. With just our rifles, Ida and I dove into the gully and hurried down the hill. By this time the bull had made his way to the pool and was standing in water half-way up his ribs. At the base of the hill we were out of sight of the bull as we moved toward him. A low ridge, perhaps six feet high, kept us hidden.

I whispered in Ida's ear, "Are you ready?"

She just nodded her head.

I whispered, "We're going to sneak up onto this ridge. He won't see us, but he'll hear us, and run out to the other side onto dry ground. When he gets there, he's going to stop and look back to see what spooked him. That's when you pop him in the lungs. OK?" Again she nodded her head.

Slowly, I raised my head above the fringe of brush. The bull's antler tips, still covered in velvet, were less than fifty feet away. I reached over and grasped Ida's arm and, as I quietly moved forward, pulled her with me. We could see most of his antlers and part of his back. We stopped before the crest and marvelled at his incredible size. He was only about forty feet away.

Ida looked as if she was about to have a heart attack. I felt much the same, as the rush of adrenaline nearly knocked me out. I was sure that the bull could hear my heart pounding.

Finally, it was time to move. I scuffed my boot lightly on the brush. That's all it took. The big bull slowly turned his massive head our way, then turned away, and quietly moved toward the opposite bank. As he started up the steep bank he suddenly kicked it into high gear, throwing mud all around. Then, just as suddenly, he turned left and stopped broadside. There he stood, glaring at us from thirty yards away.

At Ida's shot, he wheeled away and in the next instant I placed a shot behind his ear. He immediately landed on his brisket and bounced over on to his right side. His neck broken, he was snorting violently and kicking great clods of dirt and moss past me, as I ran around behind him. Quickly, I ran up and put the gun barrel to his neck and — 'click'. As I jumped back and worked the bolt open I was suddenly aware of Ida laughing. This time, I watched the magazine as the shell fed into the chamber. Again, I jumped in and 'crack'. The big bull instantly stiffened, then slowly began to relax.

I looked over at Ida and she was doubled over in laughter with tears running down her face. Needless to say the 'Bwana' was insulted at this display of gross insubordination. I grabbed my lovely wife and gave her a big kiss. "Good work honey! You've just filled our freezer!"

We could hear the hoots of our kids from the mountainside, as they charged recklessly down the steep slope. When they got to the bull, they couldn't believe how big he was. They were all talking at the same time.

"Dad," Mike said, "that was awesome! We got to see the whole thing!"

I took out the camera and set up for a photo. At this point I noticed that I'd already exposed slide #24 on a roll of 24 slide film. I must be Irish. When I flicked the film advance lever the frame moved to 25.

"OK guys, let's do this right, we've only got one shot left." I said, "This could be the best family portrait we'll ever take!"

First, I seated Ida on the front shoulder, holding her rifle, and one antler. Then Debbie sat on the ribs. Beside her, Mike sat on the belly holding my .243, and Chuck parked on the hind quarters. I focussed very carefully and set the aperture. Then, without kicking the tripod, I pushed the timer, and ran back between Debbie and Ida.

Before the bull stiffened up, we needed to get him over on his back. After a lot of grunting and struggling we eventually did just that. I soon had all the opening cuts done and the whole family went to work with skinning knives. While they were skinning I got rid of the four legs. With the bull skinned part way, it would be easier to gut. The very second I got both hands inside the moose, every black fly in the country took the opportunity to attack. As I worked, Ida kept slapping me with her jacket to keep them out of my face and hair. Finally, with a mighty heave, a whole truck load of fat and innards rolled out onto the tundra. With everyone's help, we eventually had him skinned, cut up, and piled for cooling.

We placed the fillets in a meat bag, lashed the antlers to my pack frame and headed for camp. It was only a mile, and thankfully, downhill. When we arrived, Dodd and Trudy were there to hear about the big adventure. He didn't pull a sneak on the other bull, because he'd lost sight of him, and didn't want to spook him out of the country.

Fig 16:
"This could be the best family portrait we'll ever take!"

The next morning, all seven of us headed up the hill for a load of meat. Before long, we were on our way back down with far too much weight on our backs. Mike had a cheap prospector's bag on his back. It was stuffed full of liver, tongue, heart and kidneys. After a rest break on a steep grassy slope, he struggled to get on his feet. He gritted his teeth and leaned forward into the straps. As the load passed over centre it hit him in the back of the head and he turned a complete somersault. Slightly disoriented, he simply said, "Wow!"

Struggling to our feet, we all helped Mike up and away we went. For the rest of the hunt we relaxed and enjoyed ourselves. The kids got to light their camp fire as we heated up rocks for the sweat lodge, and got cleaned up. Mike and Chuck, with their .22's, dedicated the rest of the trip to protecting us from a wild band of ptarmigan. In the end we all fared quite well.

•••

7

The Family that Hunts Together, Grunts Together...

*O*nce again, the principal and teachers are upset as the wild and savage Fergusons pull their kids out of school. Although it is early September, and they've only been back in school for a few days, priorities are priorities.

Our gear had been packed and the floatplane booked for weeks. On our day of departure, it took only minutes to throw everything in our trusty-rusty Datsun pick-up and point her north.

Five hours later, we were having a relaxing visit at the Bradford house in Dease Lake, where we would stay the night. The weather didn't look too promising, but the BC-Yukon planes were still on schedule; that was a plus.

Ray and Colleen Sande had moved all of their planes from Watson Lake to Dease, where they built a beautiful log home at the float base. In early fall Ray and his son, Ernie, were kept busy flying from daylight to dark. From early summer until late July, they were moving everything from fishermen and hikers to freight for numerous mining companies. From the time the sheep season opened on the first of August until the lower lakes began to freeze up in October, they were usually booked solid flying hunters. For this reason, I had booked our flight well in advance.

Early the next morning, Sherry had coffee boiling and breakfast on the way. Hospitality is her game as she and husband, Myles, run one of the finest guide-outfitting operations in the north. As I enjoyed my first cup of coffee, Ray was already on top of his Otter sweeping the frost off the wings.

By the time the kids were finished breakfast it was time to drive down and load the plane. I had booked the Beaver to fly us out and the Otter to fly us back in, as I expected to have a big load of meat. Since the Beaver was booked up, he offered to fly us out in the Otter at Beaver rate. What luxury! Our little pile of gear barely covered the floor of this monster. With the greatest of care, Ray made sure that each of the kids and Ida had a seat with a view. Mike was the last to be seated, right at the freight door.

Ray said, "Okay, now do up your seatbelt," which Mike did. "There," said Ray, "are you ready to go?"

Mike looked around and asked, "Where's the puke bags?"

At this we all burst out laughing. "There you go, Ray," I laughed, "how's that for a vote of confidence?"

Within fifteen minutes, we'd taxied way down the lake and Ray had a look around for other aircraft. All looked well, so it was up with the water rudders and on with the power.

It should be explained at this point, for someone who has never flown in a de Havilland Otter, that the take-offs on floats are an exhilarating experience. When the floats break free of the water, you are pressed firmly back in your seat by the sudden acceleration.

Within twenty minutes, we were closing in on our hunting area, and I liked what I saw. I'd chosen a series of lakes high on a plateau at the edge of timberline. All the lakes were interconnected by wide, grassy meadows. The few scattered patches of timber were mostly balsam, where a big tree would be twenty feet high and ten inches at the stump.

Ray banked the Otter to give me a good look at the area, and I pointed to a patch of timber not too far from the eastern shore of the longest lake. That was all Ray needed; he got to work setting up for the landing. A quick look in the back told me we'd need to feed Mike his breakfast again. Within fifteen minutes, we were standing on the grassy hillside watching Ray take off. He was soon out of sight across the plateau and the land fell silent again.

"Alright guys," I said, "let's concentrate on being as quiet as possible until after we get a moose."

The weather was threatening to get ugly, so we went in search of the perfect campsite. I couldn't believe it: there wasn't a flat spot anywhere. Finally, with a particularly miserable looking storm coming straight out of the west, I dove into a thick patch of balsam. With a quick look around, I announced: "This will have to do, guys. At least we can hang our big tarp and set up under it."

We all headed for the lake and shouldered a load of gear. By the time we got back with the second load, the first big drops of rain were arriving. I quickly grabbed a long piece of rope and, standing on a grub box, tied it as high as I could to a sturdy balsam. Then, I stretched it out and tied it to another one twenty feet away. With the whole family helping, we unfolded the 18' x 20' tarp and pulled it over the rope, tying it off at four corners. We were out of the rain.

The storm went by, and we trimmed up our camp with the axe and swede saws. Soon, our fly was set up properly with our two dome tents and kitchen safe and dry under it. With the camp readied, Debbie and the boys got antsy, so I sent them down to the lake, one hundred yards below, to pack water. By the time they got back, Ida had a snack ready for them.

The sun was breaking through here and there, so we all dressed warm and climbed the little hill behind camp. It was a perfect spot — a high grassy point just two hundred yards above our camp. From this vantage point, we could see most of the plateau for miles around. We began at once to spot moose all around us. First, there was a little bull on a small lake two miles southeast. Then a little bull swam across the north end of our long, skinny lake. About three miles to the east, we could barely make out a lone cow caribou through the spotting scope. In the same direction, but a mile closer, a cow and calf moose put in a brief appearance.

Late in the afternoon, another storm rolled through, driving us back to camp. After dinner, even though it had now become bitterly cold, we moved back up to our lookout point. There was only an hour of daylight left, and we were determined not to waste it. We spotted more moose in the distance, but that late in the day we needed one close in.

About the time it was too late to do anything but head for camp, I caught a movement. It was a monster bull moose moving slowly through the balsam across the southern tip of our lake. He was five hundred yards off and moving deeper into the timber. It was a very encouraging moment.

I crawled out into a winter wonderland at daylight the next morning and put water on for coffee. Then, I stepped out into the open for a little squint around. When the water was hot, I made myself a cup of coffee and coaxed Ida out of bed. Before long, the kids were standing out in the snow drinking hot chocolate while Ida got their breakfast ready. We didn't move very far from the kitchen. When the kids got bored, I sent them down to inflate the zodiac.

By mid-morning, when the snow was nearly gone, we pushed through the thick arctic birch to our lookout point. I spotted two bull moose beyond the end of a lake to the south of us. According to my map, they were over three miles away, about a half-mile from the far shore in scattered willows. If I got one there, we could carry it to the lake, throw it in the zodiac and paddle to the north end of the lake. From there, it was only a half-mile pack to camp.

I told Ida and the kids, "If I get one of them, grab all your packs and come help me." I left them the spotting scope so they could watch the performance, and away I went. By the time I was halfway down the lake, I could see them quite well with the naked eye as they fed through the willows. But then, they bedded down out of sight. I picked a landmark and carried on. At about a hundred yards from where I thought they were, I still couldn't see them. The willows were over twelve feet high, and scattered. I was moving dead slow, one quiet step at a time. As I moved from behind a thick willow clump, I spotted something dark. At about fifty yards, I sorted through the mess with my bino's. Then I saw a velvet covered antler palm. By the way it was curved, I judged he was facing away.

I continued quietly with a gentle breeze in my face. As I rounded another willow, I came face to face with the other bull. He was bedded facing toward me with his eyes closed. His velvet-covered antlers were about fifty-seven inches across and he was fat as a pig. The last willow bush between us was twenty feet in front of me. I could see through it, but I didn't want to shoot through it.

Holding my rifle in my left hand, I lifted my bino's with the right and looked for his eyes. They were still closed, so I took a careful step to the right. Then I could see the other bull, and he was a monster. His antlers were well over sixty inches across and his neck was massive. Although he was behind a small willow, it looked like I might get a shot through.

As I slid my bino's inside my open shirt, all hell broke loose. The bull facing me suddenly snorted and leapt out of his bed and charged to my right, with the big bull hot on his heels. I jumped back, looking for a shooting lane, but all I could see were the tops of their massive antlers as they raced away.

Suddenly, I saw the big guy's neck and I shot, with no result. Then, I saw his head again, angling away at forty yards. I tried to plant one in the back of his skull but saw a splash of white from the base of his left antler. It was an empty feeling. I just stood and watched as his antler tips headed west through the high willows.

At three hundred yards, partly in the open, he stopped broadside and looked back to see what had caused all the commotion. With my bino's, I got a good look at him. He was an awesome sight as he turned and trotted away. I was happy for him, but my freezer was still empty. I turned and headed for camp.

On my return, I was interrogated mercilessly by the kids. They had watched the entire drama unfold from the lookout point. They sat, hanging on my every word, as I related the adventure to them.

Fig 17:
Ida with the antlers and skull of a caribou bull that didn't survive the rut.
(Note: These tremendous antlers had a "Boone and Crockett" score of 446.)

After dinner, Mike and Debbie got into a wild and wooly wrestling match out on the front lawn. They closely resembled a wolf and wolverine locked in mortal combat. Chuckie was smart; he stayed back out of the way and watched the skin and hair fly. At one point, they landed upside down in a thick patch of arctic birch. Debbie had Mike in a headlock, but he had her standing right on her head. We moved in close for a better look. Debbie snarled: "Don't break us up! I can get out of this!"

And she did. With a mighty kick of both hind legs she launched herself out of the bush. They both lost their grip in her violent lunge, but by that time they were too played out to scrap any more. We headed for the kitchen, where Ida whipped up a round of hot chocolate for everyone.

That night, as I lay wide awake staring up at the tent, my amazing 20/20 hindsight came into focus. If I'd had my old .308 Savage today instead of the .243, I thought, there would be a pile of moose meat waiting for us in the morning.

It snowed during the night. By morning, it had stopped, but by the time breakfast was out of the way, it had started up again. The fog was so heavy that visibility was less than fifty yards. Late in the afternoon, the storm moved on and we stepped out for a look around. Every bush and tree was heavily loaded with sloppy, wet snow.

Slinging the rifle onto my shoulder, I said: "Come on, kids, let's go find a moose." I knocked snow off the brush with a big stick as we made our way up to the lookout point. Once on top, we spotted, on a ridge to the north, a dark trail through the arctic birch where an animal had walked, knocking off the snow in its progress. It led to the lake on the left. To the right, it ended behind a lone balsam tree. I studied the tree carefully and soon detected movement. It was a little bull — perfect.

I turned to Ida and the kids. "Okay, I'm going to pull a sneak on him. When you hear me shoot, light up a big roaring campfire. On my way back I'll come through the grass along the lake. Make sure the fire's hot, 'cause I'm going to be soaked to the skin."

On that note, I turned and hurried into the sloppy mess. He was half a mile away and I was quickly running out of shooting light. Fortunately, I broke out of the thick brush onto a long grassy opening that angled slightly to the left of the bull. I made good time there, and was soon within three hundred yards of him, as he fed broadside on the far slope. A low grassy draw separated us and I couldn't get any closer. My only chance for a rest was a lone balsam, so I forced my way into the branches around its base.

The bull, alerted by the noise I had made, was standing broadside looking my way. I cleaned the snow out of my scope and had a look through it. No good! I found a piece of Kleenex in my shirt pocket, gave the scope a quick wipe, and I was ready. As he turned to walk away, I held the crosshairs six inches above his hump and squeezed. At the shot, he bolted straight ahead to my right and stopped. Then, ever so slowly, he walked behind a patch of balsam.

I would normally wait a few minutes and then start over, but it was getting dark fast. I picked my way quietly across to where he was standing when I shot. I found no blood until the spot where he stopped the first time. Then, there was plenty of it. I followed the trail slowly, and there he was, on his side behind the patch of balsam. I quickly placed the insurance shot and it was time to go to work. Within ten minutes, he was dressed and propped open to cool. I washed my arms in the snow, put my jacket back on and grabbed my rifle.

I kept to the north side of the draw as I made my way toward the lake in the closing darkness. Twenty minutes later, I was southbound on a trail along the shore. I saw flashlights before long, moving around up on the grassy slope. A little yell and the kids all came running toward me in the dark. "We got a big fire going for you, Dad," one of them said.

"Good!" I answered. "My knees are completely numb!"

The fire was fantastic. I stood right in front of it, took off all my wet clothes and put on dry ones. The kids asked a million questions and I answered them all. In celebration, we sat up extra late and drank hot chocolate by the fire.

Morning found us once again looking out over a fresh blanket of snow. Since we weren't going to be back until late afternoon, we all had a big breakfast.

By the time we were ready to go, the sun was out and the snow was melting fast. We threw all of our gear into the little zodiac and paddled up the lake. In no time, we were pulling the raft up onto the grass. The kids were excited as they put on their pack frames.

It seemed funny that on the way back to the moose there was none of the excitement of the night before, no falling into big holes or walking face-first into sharp sticks. We even found a slight trace of a trail to follow. Our arrival at the moose was also uneventful. No grizzly bears or wolf packs to fight off. After a few photos, I cut off the lower legs and did the opening cuts. Then I stood back and photographed the process as Ida and the kids went to work with their skinning knives.

When the skinning was complete, I removed the front and hindquarters on one side. Then, while he was still on his side, I boned out the back strap from neck to hipbone. After that, we turned him over onto the hide and did the same on the other side. Next, with the hatchet, I cut out the brisket and ribs. This left only the fillets, which were now easy to get at.

We took a breather before loading the packs. First, I loaded Ida's pack with a front shoulder and side of ribs. Then, I loaded Mike's pack exactly the same way. In Debbie's pack went the liver, heart and kidneys. Chuckie got both the back straps and fillets. Finally, I loaded my heavy aluminum frame with the two hindquarters and the tongue for good measure.

By this time my back was sore so we all sat back and rested for a while. All the while, Mike kept looking at his pack — he didn't say a word. He was nine years old and weighed just sixty pounds. His pack was around ninety pounds and he knew it.

After a good rest we were ready to go, so I lifted Chuckie's pack and he slid into it. Then, I lifted Debbie's and she was into hers. I lifted Ida's next and she slid into the straps and took the weight with a groan.

Now, for Mike. I lifted his pack and he quickly got into the straps.

Fig 18:
"Ida and the kids went to work with their skinning knives…"

"OK, Dad, let me have it." he said as he braced his legs. I let him take some of the weight and he staggered a bit.

"Have I got it all?" he asked.

"Not yet."

"OK," he said, "Let me have it all." I slowly released the pack and heard the wind being forced out of his lungs.

"Get your hands under the frame, Mike, and lift up." I said "That'll help keep your shoulders from going numb."

I sat down quickly and got into my pack. As I rolled toward my belly, Ida and Chuckie pushed on the pack until it was on top of me. With their help, I struggled to my hands and knees, crawled forward, and up the side of a big rock. In this way I managed to get to my feet.

"Go!" was all I could say as Ida led the way toward the lake. Under the heavy load I couldn't look up but I could see Mike's little feet just ahead of me as he struggled along under his load.

It was only a quarter of a mile to the lake, but the trip certainly tested the mettle of the Ferguson family. Sure, we could have taken two smaller loads, but that would have made far too much sense.

•••

8
Glacier Billy...

It was almost noon. I had just spent the entire morning getting gear together for my annual deer and duck-hunting trip to Merritt. As I sat in my living room relaxing, I looked up at the snow-covered mountaintops. It was the fifth of October and there wasn't a cloud in the sky. What was I doing around the shack on a day like this? I should be out there somewhere chasing a goat.

Then, I remembered a bunch of nannies and kids I'd seen a few days before. They were across a glacier near the end of an old mining road. If I was going to try for a billy, I'd better get it done. Two weeks later there would likely be three feet of snow up there, and I was leaving for Merritt in the morning. With no time to waste, I threw my pack frame, spotting scope and bino's into the front seat of my new 1983 Toyota 4x4, then I grabbed my trusty .243 and headed out the door. After a quick stop at Hub's Pharmacy to tell Ida what was happening, I was on my way up the valley.

Few places in the world match the beauty of the Stewart area when the sun shines, and this was undoubtedly one of the very best days the country had to offer. The snow had pushed its way down just below timberline, so I expected to find the goats slightly concentrated near the bottom edge of it.

Turning off the highway, I locked my hubs and pushed my mirrors back against the doors. This is where a small pick-up really shines. The big guys keep the alders pushed back enough so that the little guys can make it through easily.

Near the end of the road, in a high rugged valley, I stopped to glass the far mountainside. Just above the snow line was a group of fourteen nannies and kids. Further glassing revealed a large-bodied goat feeding to the right and farther up in the scattered timber. At the moment, he was out on a grassy avalanche path. I could plainly see through the scope that he was a nice billy.

The only problem I had was finding a way over there. A high, jagged ridge ran down the center of the valley and petered out in a deep alder-choked canyon to my lower right. Not wanting to tackle the alders and devil's club, I made the only other choice, climb up and over the ridge.

I got into my pack frame and was checking out the slope above, looking for the best route up, when, out on the horizon stepped a goat.

It was a young billy, about a year and a half old with seven-inch horns. He was quite a sight as he studied me from three hundred yards above. The wind on top of the ridge was blowing furiously, and his beard was blowing straight out sideways. He must have been proud of his brand new winter coat as he stood there, sparkling clean in the mid-afternoon sun.

It was 2:00 PM as I headed up an avalanche path towards the little billy. The chill wind blowing down the valley from the west helped to keep me cool as I climbed. Twenty minutes later I was on top of the razor-edged ridge, where the little billy had been, looking for an easy route down to the glacier. The wind seemed to blow right through me, so I wasted no time in getting started. A thick alder slide looked as good as any; over the edge I went. Alders are a man's best friends when going downhill over cliffs and waterfalls, but they're bad news when you're trying to climb.

I was doing fine for the moment, as I grabbed a stout alder and lowered myself backward over the first cliff. About fifteen feet down, my alder was now only as big around as my finger, so I swung over and grabbed a new one where it grew out of a crack in the rock. I made my way in this manner down to where a few balsam were growing. The going became easier and I was soon sitting at the edge of the glacier, glassing the big billy. He was bedded down and looking straight down the valley to my right. At roughly six hundred yards I didn't want to make too much lateral movement, or he might spot me.

I sat shivering behind a big rock for over an hour. The wind blowing down the glacier, though not as strong as that up on the ridge, was much colder. By the time the billy decided to get up and feed I was so stiff I could barely walk.

The toe of the glacier where I was about to cross was strewn with large jagged boulders. I watched the big billy closely through my bino's. When he lowered his head to feed, I moved closer to another rock and stopped. I watched him until he lifted his head up and looked around. When he lowered his head again, I moved.

I'd somehow crossed the three hundred yards of rubble and ice undetected, and I was directly below him at the bottom of the same avalanche path he was feeding on. Before going any farther, I picked a landmark to home in on once I was up there. (Mountainsides have a nasty habit of looking much different once you're on them.) The point I'd picked was a large round boulder embedded in the center of the avalanche path, about eighty yards below the billy.

I started up the steep slope, losing sight of him behind the many humps and rock ledges. I soon had to stop and make a few changes. I took my rifle and pack frame off and lashed my rifle firmly onto the frame. That way I could climb on all fours and make much better time.

A shallow wash hid me, as I climbed the last ninety yards to the round boulder. Once safely under it, I quietly removed the pack and untied my rifle. With the rifle ready and leaning against the boulder, I took out my bino's and peeked over the boulder. He was gone. I couldn't believe my eyes. He must have bedded down again. The base of a high overhanging cliff came to a point about ninety yards above to my left. His bed was right at the tip of this point, at the edge of the timber. I looked up into the deepening shadows at the base of the cliff and saw nothing. I swept the base of the cliff one more time. I saw two eyes, but looking over my bino's I still couldn't see them. With the help of the bino's, they soon returned to view. This time I picked out a landmark. Finally, with the naked eye, I spotted him. He was lying in his bed; in the deep shadows he blended in perfectly with the light gray rock bluff.

I studied him, again through the bino's. He appeared to be looking directly at me as he chewed his cud, but he was actually looking over me and down the valley. His jet-black horns were impressive. They were heavy at the bases and carried their weight well back toward the tips. He was obviously quite comfortable in his heavy October coat.

It was 5:00 PM and I had less than two hours of daylight left — time to make a move. I slid my bino's inside my open shirt and brought the .243 up over the edge of the boulder. He was lying facing toward me, so I put the cross hairs where I could hit the top of the heart.

At the shot, he jumped up with his rump against the cliff and looked back to his right along the mountainside. Then, he turned broadside and looked along the other side to his left. I quietly worked the bolt and put one through both lungs. He didn't even flinch, but stood there calmly looking around. Suddenly, his knees buckled and he began a slow end-over-end roll down the mountain toward me.

I leaned my rifle against the rock and scrambled across the slide to intercept him. Through some stroke of luck, he stopped on a narrow bench. After a minute or so, I went back, grabbed my rifle and pack, and climbed up to him. He was a beauty, a big rugged animal totally suited to the harsh environment he lived in. His lofty coat was nearly ten inches thick along his back, and his fancy leggings were fully grown out around his front legs. With great difficulty, I dragged him across the slide path about twenty feet to the only flat spot on the entire mountainside, cleaned him up with snow, and took a few photos.

91

Fig 19:
"The billy was totally suited to the harsh environment he lived in."

The knife work was finished less than an hour later and the real work was about to begin. I had to return with a heavy load of meat around the toe of the jagged ridge through heavy alder and devil's club. I arrived back at my pick-up in the black dark, five hours after I'd left it.

•••

9
Spatsizi Caribou...

My hunting partner, Dodd Hareuther, and I had kicked around the idea of a Spatsizi caribou hunt for a few years. I could never make it because of the nature of my work. The rest of the time, I was just too crippled to go on such a demanding hunt. Eventually, after my third back operation I was in good enough shape to go, so we applied for the limited entry draw. With my back fused in three places, I felt better than I had in years. I felt even better when the news came in the mail that we had been drawn. We booked our flight with Trans-Provincial Airlines for the middle of September. With our holidays booked and our gear packed, we were ready to go.

On the day we were scheduled to fly, the wind was blowing furiously, as a high pressure system forced its way into northern BC. I was happy about the clear dry weather, but dreaded the impending flight. Our pilot was Murray Woods, a wily old veteran with plenty of hours logged dodging northern BC's rugged mountains. Whenever certain passengers appeared a little nervous, Murray would comfort them by pretending to fall asleep at the controls.

Our takeoff from Eddontenajon Lake was a rush to say the least. Once the Beaver broke free of the choppy water, we shot two thousand turbulent feet almost straight up over the mountains to the east. By the time we had crossed the Klappan River, Dodd looked like a big spider with his arms and legs all over the back of the plane trying to hold our gear down. At one point, a cooking pot got loose from the security netting and chased us around the cabin. By the time we landed on Cold Fish Lake our breakfast was, as they say, in the bag.

After stowing our base camp gear in a cabin, we wasted no time getting into our packs and heading north up the old horse trail. We hiked for several miles without stopping for anything but air and water. On these brief rest breaks we would take the time to glass the mountains around us for any sign of caribou. All we managed to spot was one lonely cow and calf across the valley.

By late afternoon, we had reached the summit of the horse trail where it turned east down a long sparsely timbered valley. Our plans were to cross the upper end of this valley and hunt the mountains to the north. We crawled out of our packs in a boulder patch near the horse trail and got out the spotting scope. We were not long in spotting caribou. Directly across the valley to the north, a fine fat bull grazed along the mountain-side with his harem of nine cows and calves. Satisfied that we would be into more caribou soon, we got back into our packs and went looking for water and a campsite. A quarter of a mile south, around the mountain-side, we found a little spring and set up camp.

As we set up the tent, we were treated to the antics of several hundred willow ptarmigan in their noisy cackling flight to their roosting area--our camp. They poured in from every direction for over an hour, landing in groups from six to twenty or more. We were camped on the upper edge of a mile wide strip of wolf willow, which is the willow ptarmigan's fa-vourite roosting habitat.

A fox must have gotten into the chicken coop during the night, as, on several occasions, we were jolted awake by the sudden squawking and flapping of ptarmigan in full scale panic. At the first hint of daylight, we were awakened by the raucous voices of our fine feathered neighbours as they prepared for their morning flight. Judging by the amount of noise erupting from the willows, I guessed they were doing their sit-ups and wing stretches. Then, as if a cannon had been fired, they all took off at the same time headed for their favourite feed areas.

There was not a chicken in sight by the time Dodd and I crawled out of the tent. The blue sky promised a nice day, as the sun peeked over the eastern horizon. We slung our sleeping bags out on the rocks to dry and strolled around, eating trail mix and sipping orange juice, as we tried to work out a few kinks. Dodd took a walk down through the wolf willow and found fairly conclusive evidence that some of our former neighbours were now in chicken heaven. "Ferg," he said, "there's piles of white feath-ers all over the place down here."

Before loading up our packs we checked out the far side of the valley with the spotting scope. A small herd of caribou fed in the bottom of the high pass to the north. Farther down the valley to the east, a bull moose had a cow and a calf pushed up into a high willow-choked basin on the north side. He'd try to keep her there until she came into oestrus.

With our packs loaded, we worked our way down toward a big grassy meadow, where we hoped to find a horse trail up the north side. In the far corner of the meadow we found exactly that. As we worked our way up into the high pass, we kept to the south side as the center looked too wet. We soon found the reason why. Incredibly, there were beaver dams even there above timberline with nothing for materials but four-foot-high willows.

We negotiated our way through the dams and found ourselves north-bound on the east side of the pass. Two miles across the tundra, we came across a clear fast running spring pouring right out of the mountain side. Forty yards from the spring was a flat bottom depression where we could pitch our dome tent out of the wind. We wasted no time in setting up camp so that we could have a look around. After glassing all of the west side of the pass and spotting only a few scattered caribou, we grabbed our packs and rifles and headed up the east side behind camp. The grassy slopes made for easy walking. In some places the benches were so flat one could likely have landed a plane.

At a prominent point we stopped to glass. A young caribou bull had been following us up the slope since we left camp. He was a long way back, so he hadn't identified us as humans yet. When he dropped out of sight in a dip, we ran and hid behind a big boulder. As he came back into view at three hundred yards he seemed disturbed that he couldn't see us. On he came, nearly straight for the rock we were hiding behind. I got my camera ready and, as he passed within thirty yards, snapped his picture. He jumped to the side at the click of the camera and trotted away with his tail pointed straight up. Soon, feeling safe, he stopped to see what spooked him. After studying us for a while, he suddenly reared up on his hind legs and trotted away. This time, he went non-stop over the summit a mile to the east.

We stayed and glassed for another hour, spotting a few scattered caribou, then headed back to the camp for supper. For our evening meal, we carried Ichiban soup mix crunched up and repackaged in Ziploc bags. We also had beef jerky and fruit leather. For dessert we had a chocolate coated granola bar. All of this and plenty of water sent us to bed content.

We weren't in bed ten minutes when we heard the most god-awful wailing out on the tundra, and it seemed to be getting closer. We jumped into our clothes and crawled out of the tent. The light was fading quickly, so we load our rifles and headed toward the commotion. Before long we discovered the source of all the excitement. A wildly in love young bull moose was running back and forth on the tundra trying to keep a not-so-in-love cow, nearly twice his size from making it to the valley bottom to the south. When they stopped in a low spot, we jumped on the chance and ran right up to within thirty yards of them. The cow saw us right away and nearly flattened the little bull on her way out. This time, as the cow rushed toward the valley, the bull followed quietly. Dodd and I turned and headed for camp, thankful it wasn't a sow grizzly with three cubs.

It was daylight and the air was cold and damp. I sat up and unzipped the tent. To my surprise four inches of fresh snow covered the ground. I got dressed as quietly as possible, trying not to wake Dodd until I was out of the tent. There was a reason for this. One look at his morning face can ruin a person's breakfast.

Once outside in the brisk wind I zipped up the tent and said, "Dodd, are you awake?"

He answered, "Hrummph."

"Good ," I said "I'm going for a quick look while you get dressed." I carefully glassed the area immediately around the tent, then climbed up out of the little bowl. Patches of thick fog were blowing across the tundra from the west. The light was still poor, but I soon spotted a herd of caribou feeding across the pass to our north. They were over a mile away, but I could make out a mature bull with his striking white mane.

As soon as Dodd came out of the tent, we grabbed our packs and rifles and headed north along the east side of the pass. We were soon warmed up and shaking off the chill. A narrow bench with a fringe of wolf willow along it's edge protected us from view as we move along the mountainside. The herd was feeding toward us and as they got into the bottom of the pass, broke into a run straight up the slope below us. They were only four hundred yards away moving toward our left and we could see the bull fairly well. When they dropped out of sight in a low spot, we took advantage and moved about one hundred yards to a prominent hump below.

Now we were down in the arctic birch where we had a bit more cover. From the crest of the hump we saw nothing. We were facing directly into the wind, and glassing brought tears to our eyes. Suddenly, from behind a bench below, a yearling cow ran into the open and began to feed. Before long the whole happy herd of nine cows and calves poured into the open. As one cow strayed downhill, the bull ran from behind the bench and diverted her back toward the herd. From two hundred yards, we got a good look at him and I liked what I saw. His antlers were fairly heavy and sported a single big shovel. His bez, the beams directly above the shovel, were heavy and palmated. The tops had the prerequisite six points, and to top it off he was as fat as a pig.

I looked at Dodd and said, "Do you want him?"

He said, "No."

I looked at the bull one more time and said "I think I want him."

He looked at me in surprise. "Really?"

"Yup," I said, "he's a nice bull."

The herd had moved out of sight below a low bench to our left. They were headed roughly in the direction of our camp to the south. By the time I hiked down to the edge of the bench, the program had changed. My bull and his cows had run smack into the harem of another bull. This herd was in a dip below us the whole time. After a bit of frantic charging around, the bulls got their ladies sorted out without having to go to war. My bull was busy ushering his cows back down the hill toward the creek bottom. He was two hundred yards away, but running around too much for me to attempt a shot.

The other bull, meantime, was standing on a prominent point watching their quick departure. He was only a hundred and fifty yards to my left, but didn't know I was near. He appeared to be about a four year old bull. He was not as big in the body as the bull I was after and his antlers weren't as heavy. What was good about this guy was his genetics. His antlers in a year would be absolutely breathtaking. He had double shovels, fine bez points and his tops were slightly palmated, with lots of long points on each side.

My next challenge was to get past him and his cows without spooking them. Backing into a slight depression, I worked my way to the right and down the hill behind a fringe of arctic birch. I ran out of cover at an open, grassy spot. A large boulder thirty yards away in the open looked like my only chance. To the left, all I could see was a single yearling cow bedded down less than sixty yards away. I got down and crawled in the snow, dragging my pack with one hand and cradling my rifle in the other. Just as I got to the rock, she spotted my movement. I was pinned down. She stared a me for twenty minutes until finally deciding it was only her imagination. By then, I was chilled to the bone and desperate to get moving again.

The cow lay her head down facing away, as if she had read my mind. I wasted no time in getting behind a strip of arctic birch. Once behind cover again, I looked back at Dodd. He was watching me with the bino's. I gave him the thumbs up and dropped over the edge out of sight into another low spot. Nearing the creek bottom, I carefully climbed the side of a little ridge. There they were, about four hundred yards away, feeding right up the middle of the pass.

Just then, the sun broke through and warmed my aching bones. It would only be a few minutes before every caribou in the country was bedded down. A quick glance up the hill showed the young bull and his cows all relaxing in the sun. The big bull and his cows finally fed their way out of sight up the right side of the creek bottom and out onto the gently sloping tundra. Now I was free to march up the creek without them spotting me.

As I picked my way up the creek, I glanced back to my left and noticed that the young bull had spotted me. He rounded up his cows and was herding them straight over the mountain to the east. This gave Dodd a chance to move down the mountain side for a better view of the action. With the creek bottom barely deep enough to hide me, and a wide marshy area opening up on my right, I had run out of cover. Peeking over the low bush, I spotted the herd on the far side of the marsh. They had been bedded for about half an hour, soaking up the warmth of the sun.

A large flat topped rock lay nearly flush with the tundra fifty yards ahead. This would make a great shooting bench. I noticed some of the cows were up feeding. With a sense of urgency, I removed my pack. Carrying the pack in my left hand and the .243 in my right, I moved quickly toward the rock. I was back on my belly for the last fifty feet, trying to protect my rifle and drag my pack without making too much noise. Finally, at the rock I took another look. This time all of the cows and calves were on their feet. The bull was three hundred yards away and ready to get up. With a bit of squirming I manoeuvred the pack onto the rock and slid the rifle into position. I opened the bolt, quietly fed a round into the chamber and flipped the safety on.

The bull stood up like a big lazy horse, stretching his back and arching his neck. If I didn't try him now he would be gone across three miles of open tundra. He was standing perfectly broadside facing to my left as I eased into position. Looking at him through the scope, I got that familiar feeling of confidence that comes from all the years of success with the same old rifle. Even after I cranked the 4x12 Leopold up to full power and flipped off the safety he still looked a mile away. I held about a foot above his back, let my breath out and started the squeeze.

At the shot, the bull took one quick step forward and froze. I watched him for about fifteen seconds before he moved at all. Then, with his head hanging slightly down his antlers began to tip slowly to the left. In typical caribou manner he just tipped, stiff-legged, over to his side like an old saw horse — a perfect lung shot. The cows fed quietly up the gentle slope, not seeming to have heard the shot. They didn't even notice the absence of their late husband. So much for family ties in the wild kingdom.

I spotted Dodd down the creek, on top of a bushy ridge about 400 yards across the pass. He was watching me through his bino's. I gave him the thumbs up signal and he waved back and stood up. I slowly worked my way around the soggy ground toward my bull, running through the feelings that go through a person after taking the life of an animal he admires and respects. I was grateful to be alone with my thoughts.

I finally reached my bull and I was impressed. He didn't stink at all from the rut. He was fat as a hog with a flowing white mane. His dark legs ended in a thin fringe of silver around the top of each hoof. His dark chocolate coloured face was picture-perfect, with his silver nose hairs sparkling in the bright sunlight. His antlers were heavy and well-formed with a single big shovel and two massive bez. The tops were not big, but nicely formed.

It was time for breakfast. I got out my trail mix and water bottle and sat back beside my bull. The wind was still quite strong out of the west, but the sun was warming things up considerably.

When Dodd arrived, he was all smiles. "Wow!", he said "He's nicer than I thought." He reached out to shake my hand and said "Good work partner. He's going to look good up on your wall."

"Yep," I said, "and the meat is going to look good in my freezer."

We took our time inspecting the bull again, trying to imagine how good the meat would be. It's hard to beat good caribou meat. On the other hand, once heavily into the rut, there is nothing that will gag a maggot quicker than caribou. We moved the bull into position, got out the camera and tripod and took a whole mess of photos. Next, we did the opening cuts for the cape. While Dodd worked at skinning off the cape, I started skinning one side of the back end.

At some point during the skinning process, I had stopped to sharpen my knife and was admiring the scenery. A bit of movement caught my eye on the mountainside across the pass. "Look Dodd." I said "There's a guy headed straight for our tent!" We watched as he passed about a stones throw from it without spotting it down in the little depression. Twenty minutes later he was out of sight through a high pass behind camp.

We had the cape off, the meat boned out and the antlers chopped out of the skull within an hour. We rested for awhile then put the meat in meat bags and into our packs. The cape was put into another meat bag after being washed in the creek. Once the antlers were tied onto my pack, we were ready to head for camp, which was about a mile straight across the pass to the southeast. We each took a big drink of water and filled our water bottles at the creek. I helped Dodd into his pack first, then sat down on the ground to struggle into my own. It took a determined effort, but Dodd managed to pull me to my feet.

Fig 20:
"He was fat as a hog with a flowing white mane."

Two hours later we staggered into camp and shed our heavy loads. It was mid-afternoon. We had a quick bite to eat and I spent the rest of the afternoon working on my cape — splitting the lips and turning the ears. The wind blew hard all day and was beginning to shift from the north. We were in for a big high-pressure system, which meant warm days and clear cold nights. Time to bring in the brass monkey.

Dodd spent most of the afternoon glassing the miles of rolling tundra looking for caribou that were bedded down out of the wind. We ate early in case we should be attacked by a herd of caribou before dark. We didn't have long to wait. Just above camp, a young bull and his cows drifted across the skyline on their evening feeding frenzy. Another herd materialized on the other side of the pass directly in the path of the setting sun. From two miles away, we counted more than a dozen caribou. With the spotting scope trained on the herd, I noticed a large rack coming over the ridge.

"Here comes your bull, Dodd," I announced. "He's high and wide but I can't make out his shovel and bez set up too well."

We watched the show unfold as more cows and bulls appeared on the plateau. They were all feeding except for the big bull. He just stood with his nose nearly touching the ground, as gaunt as a greyhound. The rigors of the rut had taken a toll on him. Whenever another bull got too close to one of his cows, he would suddenly rush at him, and then stand there with his head hanging down again. Soon he was off to the other side of his harem chasing another young bull.

Finally, out of daylight and on the verge of dying from hypothermia, we crawled into our tent. As well prepared as we were for the nasty weather, I wasn't ready to peel off the laundry and jump into my sleeping bag naked. In fact, I took off my boots and climbed in fully clothed. Even with my hard hat liner on I was still cold. This was turning out to be one hell of a mid-September cold snap. To make matters worse, I discovered that the feathers in my sleeping bag had migrated south and left me practically uncovered around my chest and shoulders. In contrast, Dodd settled into his fluffy new bag and slept like a baby all night.

I pulled on my boots around daylight and dragged my sorry tail out into the cold. As I straightened up my aching back, I was hit with a blast of chill air that nearly took my breath away. Not wanting to keep all this fun to myself, I called out, "Dodd, it's almost shooting light."

He sat up in his bag and looked out the door. "Hmm" he said, "Is it gonna be a nice day?"

"As long as this high pressure holds, we'll be in good shape."

As Dodd got dressed, I walked over to the creek for a drink of water. Just as I suspected, it was frozen over all the way down the mountain side. The only place to fill the water bottle was in the first two feet where it boiled out of the rocks.

Dodd and I were beginning to loosen up; we munched on our half-frozen energy bars and scanned the immediate area for signs of life. It was light enough within minutes to glass the wide plateau across the pass. There was not a caribou to be seen anywhere. I could see the remains of my bull on the far slope. We watched carefully for movement in the area, as we were not interested in a performing scene from "Dances with Grizzlies".

We were ready to go after checking all our gear and slipping into our packs. As it turned out, we would have to pass fairly close to yesterday's kill to reach the north-eastern edge of the plateau. We were fairly sure there was nothing in the area as we approach the kill, but it doesn't hurt to be cautious. So far nothing had been around. Just to make sure that something with big claws didn't set up camp too soon, we scent-marked the area, wolf style.

By the time we reached the rim of the plateau, the sun was up and it was finally warming up enough to sit and glass for awhile. It only took a minute for us to spot a herd of caribou more than a mile to the north. One showed a white mane, indicating a mature bull. However, his antlers didn't seem to stand out much, so we carried on glassing. We spotted a few more animals off to the north, but no bulls. We worked our way around the north end of the plateau, expecting any moment to spot the big bull and his entourage. An endless series of low hog backs flowed from the plateau to the wide bench below creating several quiet basins out of the wind. As the air warmed up, we expected to find them bedded in these types of places.

We had reached the north west corner of the plateau by mid-morning. It was still very windy, but had warmed up considerably. I found it hard to believe that we hadn't found the herd yet, but that's hunting. The view from up top was incredible, so we were enjoying ourselves just the same. We carried on along the western slope toward the southwest corner of the mountain, until we found a spot out of the wind. There, we could stop for lunch and have a good look around. Five miles to the south, we could see 'ptarmigan camp' where we had set up the first night out. To the west, from the lofty elevation of six thousand feet, we could see all the way to the snow-covered Coast Range.

With lunch out of the way and having spotted only a few scattered cows and calves, we decided to head for the north side again. The top of this mountain was as flat as an airport, so we headed straight across the top. The only landmarks were a few scattered boulders standing square shouldered like monuments against the skyline. We recognized one particularly oddly shaped rock as the one the caribou herd was feeding close to last evening. It seemed like a good lookout point, so I climbed to the top of it for a little look around — more tundra and boulders.

When we reached the northern edge, it was late afternoon. We were tired, thirsty and four miles from camp. In two hours the sun would be down and we had yet to spot a legal bull. Dodd looked a little dejected as we sat glassing several thousand acres of seemingly caribou-less tundra. "I wonder if they're down in the timber" he said.

"I don't think so." I answered. "This time of year, with the rut beginning, they like to stay up fairly high and in the open."

To our left, a low saddle in the plateau sloped off toward our right and fanned out to form a wide grass-covered flat. A good portion of the meadow was hidden by a prominent ridge below us that formed the eastern boundary of the basin. It was only a few hundred yards away, so we headed over toward the ridge top for a peek. On the way over, we discovered a little spring at the base of the ridge. It appeared to pick up volume considerably where it hooked left around the toe of the ridge below. We took a big drink and with our water bottles filled eased our way up the last hundred yards out on to the top of the ridge.

We still couldn't see that piece of meadow directly below us, so I stepped up on to a big boulder for a better look. Caribou! I stepped back down and turned to Dodd, "There's a few caribou there but I don't know if there are any bulls."

Suddenly, we were wired. We crawled out of our packs quietly, grabbed our rifles, bino's, spotting scope and tripod and eased out to the edge of the ridge. Right off the bat, a young bull moved out into the open on the far side of a half dozen cows. They were just two hundred yards below us. We crawled another thirty yards on our hands and knees to a slight hump, where we could have a better look. When we peeked over the edge, we were not prepared for what we saw. In an area of less than an acre, there were nearly forty caribou. Most of the cows and calves were bedded down, but all of the bulls, six or seven of them, were on their feet. They appeared to be ready to party, but the cows were pretending not to notice. One particular bull immediately caught our attention with his flowing white mane and heavily beamed, very dark antlers. Curiously, they had absolutely no palmation and looked more like elk antlers. There was little doubt that he sported the biggest headgear of this friendly gathering.

"Get ready to shoot, Dodd, while I get a count on his top points." I cranked the neck of the tripod up until I could see fairly well over the tops of the sparse tundra grasses. Focusing on the bull, I counted only four long points on the top of each side of his antlers. Unless he had a legal sticker point up there somewhere, he was not a legal bull. "Nope. It's hard to believe, Dodd but he's not going to make it."

He slowly shook his head and turned to me. "Now that's one hell of a nice bull."

"Oh well" I whispered, "He'll spread his genes one more time."

We carefully studied the other bulls and noticed that some of them, although not of trophy size, were legal with five or more points on top. Typical of young bulls, they were without the heavy white mane. If the wolves didn't get them this winter, they would be the dominant bulls next September. As we lay there enjoying the moment, I began to gaze around at the rest of the country. Through my bino's something caught my eye about two miles to the west.

Checking through the spotting scope, I made out two cows and a fantastic big bull. He was too far away for us to make out his antler configuration, but they were obviously massive.

"What do you think, Dodd?"

"I don't know partner." he said. "He's a long way off and we're running out of time."

"That's right" I answered, "We can make it there in shooting light if we put on a forced march. We'll have to cape him out and head for the timber, where we can "Siwash" it for the night. It's going to be a ball freezer and the only food we have other than that bull over there is a couple of Granola bars. Are you into it?"

"I'm into it." he said. Damn, I was hoping he wouldn't say that.

"OK, let's get moving."

We backed away from the ridge and worked our way back to our packs without spooking the herd. With our packs back on, we headed toward the top of the plateau to get well out of sight of the herd. After a few hundred yards, we swung to the west and crossed the wide saddle at a 'young' gallop. We had gone a good quarter of a mile at a fairly ferocious pace, so we stopped and sat down for a quick breather. From this angle we could see all of the herd quite easily now. The sun was low in the sky and directly behind us; they were not likely to notice us. Out of instinct, I suppose, I lifted my bino's to my eyes and had another look at them.

"Holy crap, Dodd. Take a look at the right side of the herd. It's the big bull from last night, and he's been right under our nose the whole time."

Dodd took a quick look and lit up like a Christmas tree. "C'mon partner, let's go," he said, as he dragged me unceremoniously to my feet.

Soon, we were back on the east side of the saddle and out of sight behind the little ridge. This time, we stayed to the left and worked our way down a little draw toward the bull. We crawled on our bellies out onto the edge, where we could get a better look at him. What a sight he was, resting there with his white mane flashing in the sun. Most of the cows were bedded within fifty feet of him; he was obviously still the host of this party. It would have been nice to just lie here and watch him for awhile, but we were running out of time.

I whispered to Dodd, "Go ahead crawl out as far as you can without spooking them. Make sure your bullet clears the grass or it may explode." Dodd was shooting snarly handloads out of his brand new, custom built 25-06.

He managed to crawl to a rocky little hump about thirty yards up to my right before he was finally spotted. A cow lying about ten feet in front of the big guy jumped to her feet with a snort and fixed us with 'the look'. None of the others seemed to react until she bobbed her head up and down and snorted again. It was the big bull who let out a guttural grunt as if to say, "Quiet woman, I'm trying to sleep." By then, she was working herself up into a small frenzy and the rest of the herd was beginning to pay attention. Soon, the whole herd was on its feet wondering just exactly what crawled up her skirt.

Fig 21:
"The battle to keep his cows ... had taken a terrible toll on him. "

The big bull, meantime, seemed quite content to stay right where he was until such time as he received a registered letter stating that his life was in danger. During all this foolishness, Dodd had settled in behind his rifle and had the bull perfectly broadside in his scope. He looked back at me as if to say, "Shall I shoot him while he's laying down." I nodded my head and gave him the thumbs up.

At the shot, the bull lurched forward and got his hind end up. Then, with another heave, he was up on all fours. A small blood spot indicated a perfect lung shot. Dodd looked back at me with a big grin. Within seconds, the bull's tall antlers began the slow motion tip to the left and over he went. As I walked over to shake Dodd's hand, the herd finally swung into action and circled to our right and up onto the top of the plateau. We counted them as they went over the horizon — twenty nine cows and calves and seven bulls.

We gathered our gear together and began the quiet walk down toward the bull. That familiar feeling of sadness drifted over us as we got closer, then vanished completely as we walked up to him. It appeared that we had done him a big favor, judging by the physical state he had been in. He was full of antler punctures from nose to tail including a particularly ugly hole in his flank with a chunk of severed intestine hanging out of it. The battle to keep his cows from the determined gang of young bulls had taken a terrible toll on him. He would, without a doubt, have died an agonizing death over the next few days.

The sun was close to setting, so we quickly set up the camera and took a few photos before starting the opening cuts to remove the cape. The first cut, from the top of his neck directly behind the skull along the center line to a point directly above his elbow, gave us our first good snoot full of a caribou in full rut. It takes a strong stomach to be able to skin an animal that smells that bad. It was quite a contrast to my bull, who would be fine eating, but was only a few days from stinking just as badly as this guy.

We finished the knife work and loaded up in record time. Turning our backs to yet another glorious sunset, we point our noses for camp. We didn't get very far before I noticed a bleached-out set of caribou antlers on the skyline about 200 yards above to our right. Always curious about the many different antler configurations of caribou, I told Dodd to watch out for the grizzlies and that I'd meet him in camp.

He just smiled as he turned away and said "Don't worry, partner; he'll only take one bite and spit me out."

When I got to the rack, I was amazed at its size. It had two large shovels, long palmated bez with four or five long points on each side, and heavily palmated tops with lots of long symmetrical points on both sides. He would have made it well into the record books. It's very likely he died the year before, during or shortly after the rut.

In the meantime, Dodd was nearly run over by a dozen wild-eyed, snorting cows, as they came thundering down off the top of the plateau with one of the young bulls in hot pursuit. There was suddenly bedlam on the mountain, as seven young bulls, enhanced by overflowing testosterone levels, charged all over the landscape trying desperately to gather up as many of the recently widowed cows as they could. Much to their chagrin, none of the cows seem to be ready for another permanent relationship.

As I made my way toward camp in the fading light, I was startled by a sudden loud snorting and the thundering of hooves. The same herd that had tried to run over Dodd had been turned by the bull, and was now about to grace my carcass with a lovely pattern of fresh tracks. The lead cow spotted me and slid to a stop less than thirty feet away on the opposite slope of a low ridge. The rest of the herd split left and right and came to a halt, forming a half-moon around me. It was a rare treat to be this close to a dozen bug-eyed foot-stomping, snot-blowing caribou.

The bull, his sides heaving for breath, glared at me from behind the lead cow. In less than five seconds it was all over. The cow reared up on her hind legs like a horse, let out a final snort and jumped over a calf on her right. The whole herd bolted and within a few minutes was out of sight a mile across the tundra. By the time I reached the western edge of the pass, it was nearly too dark to see. With the last pale rays of light glowing against the far side, I could just make out Dodd through my bino's. He was only a quarter mile from camp. A quick look around my kill far below revealed no sign of grizzlies.

I stopped on the upward slope an hour later to rest and get my wind. It was already bitterly cold, so I couldn't sit too long. Somewhere above me, Dodd had the water boiling for my dinner. On the chance that I was getting close to camp, I called out his name.

"Right here partner," he answered from only a few hundred yards above. I was home! My noodle soup, jerky and fruit leather tasted better than Mom's Christmas dinner that night. When our meal was out of the way, we grabbed our toothbrushes and headed for the spring. I didn't even want to imagine how cold it was going to get during the night, with the stiff north wind already burning our faces.

Getting dressed in the pre-dawn darkness was easy. I was already there. As I struggled into my frozen boots Dodd began to wake up. I unzipped the tent enough to stick my head out. Damn, it was cold. To make matters worse, a bitter wind was still blowing out of the north.

"We've got enough light to pack up, but we'll have to make it fast or we're going to freeze to death."

I opened the flap and threw all my gear out into the wind, then crawled out to face the inevitable. My guts began to tremble in shock. Swinging into gear I quickly ran around the tent to remove the fly. One good shake and all the accumulated frost was gone. The meat bags were frozen solid; we had to put them into our packs first and stuff the rest of our gear in all around them.

We had camp torn down and both packs loaded within twenty minutes. Dodd took a photo of me with my load on, and we decamped. The wind was, thankfully, at our backs. The first three miles went quite well until we hit the flats of the high valley below 'ptarmigan camp'. There we found a sunny spot out of the wind and sat down for a well- earned breakfast of granola, fruit leather and orange juice. What more could a worn out, half-frozen caribou hunter want at a time like this?

The next half mile up to the horse trail was brutal. Out of steam and in need of more drinking water, we got out of our packs and went searching. Dodd soon found a little stream where we had a big drink, filled our bottles, and lay back in the warm sun for a little snooze. It was hard to believe the contrast to the temperature three hours earlier.

The trail was downhill the rest of the way and the weather stayed dry. Eleven hours and twelve miles after leaving our spike camp, we staggered into base camp. As sorry a sight as we were, there were no two happier hunters anywhere. Dodd fell to the ground in front of our cabin and rolled out of his pack. I collapsed beside him in a tangled mess of my own, not believing we had made it. Dodd reached down and I took his hand. He pulled me to my feet and said, "Well, partner, that was one hell of a hunt." And it was. Our grinning faces told it all.

Just then, two men came out of another cabin and came down for a visit. They were Robert Werrell, and his partner, Marvin Gerow, from Burns Lake, BC. They had both gotten nice bulls as well. Robert, as it turned out, was the lone hunter that had hiked past our camp a few days back.

We all got together for a big caribou steak dinner after getting cleaned up and changing clothes. It was a treat: good food, great company and a few cold beer. If my memory serves me correctly we may have told the odd lie that night as well. I certainly hope so.

Note: Our bulls were both expertly mounted by Brittons Taxidermy in Smithers, B.C.

•••

10

Stones in a Rock Pile...

In the spring of 1992, when the BC Government issued the limited entry forms, every hunter in the province was scrambling for a copy. My older son, Mike, and his friend, Neil Rowe, applied for a group hunt for stone sheep out of Atlin. My younger son, Chuck, and I did the same. We also applied separately for caribou and mountain goat in other zones.

When our notices finally came in the mail, there was wild jubilation in the little town of Stewart — we had all been drawn for sheep and goat. First things first: we called Summit Air to reserve our flights. Mike and Neil planned their hunt for opening day on August 1st. Chuck and I planned to fly in on the same flight that would pick Mike and Neil up at the end of their hunt. That would save us a few hundred dollars. Mike would also set up base camp and leave it for us to bring home.

Chuck was sixteen at the time and this would be his first sheep hunt. Mike, on the other hand, was eighteen and this would be his fourth. Neil had been on a few good riverboat trips with his dad, Larry Rowe, and had gotten a few nice moose. For this trip Larry had been nice enough to let them use his sparkling new Ford Diesel for the fourteen-hour trip to Atlin. Chuck and I would have to be content to make the trip in my old beat-up 1983 Toyota Long-Box. I guess that's life in the 'rough' lane!

The month of July took forever to get past, then everything suddenly flew into overdrive. Two days before the season opening, Mike and Neil made the long drive. The next morning they were dropped off at our chosen lake and wasted no time setting up camp. Late in the afternoon they hiked up a horse trail to have a little look around. They were sitting near a scrubby patch of balsam glassing for sheep when a man rode up behind them on a horse. Mike recognized him right away as a young guide from the outfitters' camp at the other end of the lake.

He got down from his horse with a friendly smile and said, "Hi! I remember you! You and another guy got a nice ram here three years ago!"

"That's right," Mike said, "I was just a little guy then. I'm surprised you recognized me."

At that, they re-introduced themselves and sat down for a good visit. The guide's name was Kent, and, according to Mike, was a real nice guy. As darkness closed in, they all headed for camp to prepare for the big day.

Opening morning found Mike and Neil, shortly after daylight, sitting by the same patch of balsam glassing for rams. This time their packs were loaded for a three or four-day tour. They were sitting there only a short while when Kent and his American hunter rode up leading a packhorse. They all exchanged greetings and Kent introduced Mike and Neil to his hunter. "He's a little past middle age," Mike said, "and a first-class sportsman."

Mike and Kent held a short pow-wow to figure out where each party was going to go so they wouldn't collide somewhere on the mountain. They were sitting in a high pass with narrow valleys falling off in three directions, much like the spokes of a wagon wheel. Kent said, "Which way are you going to go, Mike?"

"I'm going to head for that saddle up there," Mike answered, pointing toward a rugged ridge across the pass to the north.

"Okay," Kent said, "We're going to work our way back around this mountain to our right." They all wished each other good luck as Kent and his hunter mounted up and rode away. Mike and Neil glassed the ridge one more time, got into their packs and headed out across the mile-wide valley.

At the creek bottom, they stopped to rest, have a drink, and re-fill their water containers. As they sat back in the grass among the scattered balsam, they instinctively glassed the ridge-top again. Rams, right on the horizon to the left! Mike got out the spotting scope and set it up on the tripod. He started counting as they slowly came into view at just over a mile. He had counted over a dozen rams, some of them legal, when he abruptly stopped. "Let's get going!" He snapped. "I don't know how many there are but we'd better get across the valley out of sight and figure out a plan!"

They managed to get out of sight behind the swell of the steep slope without being spotted. Mike said, "Let's keep going to the top of the ridge, then we'll unload our packs and go after them."

An hour of hard climbing found them taking a breather four hundred yards below the saddle. Mike glanced up the ridge and spotted movement. It was Kent and his hunter. Obviously, they had spotted the rams and crossed the little valley farther down in the timber. While Mike and Neil had been sitting watching the rams, Kent and his hunter were already partway up the other side.

Mike realized that once Kent had spotted the rams, it would have been impossible for him to ride away, given the fact that he was obligated to his hunter. They hurried to the crest of the saddle and unloaded their spike camp and food. Then, with their packs, optics and rifles, they headed up the ridge to the west. They stayed back a good distance from Kent and stayed out of sight of the rams. Mike crawled up to a boulder-strewn hump where he and Neil could watch the whole performance.

Kent and the hunter had made their way along the very rugged north face of the ridge and were slowly working their way up over the top. The rams were roaming around feeding on the south-facing slope just below the crest. By then, Mike had the spotting scope focussed and, from five hundred yards, counted twenty-one rams! At least six of them were better than full curl.

Imagine the stress this young guide must have been under as he worked his hunter into position for the shot with twenty-one sets of eyes always watching for danger. Mike and Neil had their rifles ready in case some of the rams might run their way after the shot.

When the hunter finally crawled into position, he was barely eighty yards above the unsuspecting rams. Kent, by this time, had already sized them up and whispered to his hunter which one to take. He wasted little time in getting the shot away, and in the process, suddenly jolted the whole ridge-top into a flurry of wild action. As luck would have it, none of the sheep came Mike's way. They all ran back around the top of the ridge to the west and, within a few seconds, there was not a sheep in sight.

Mike and Neil got back into their packs, grabbed their rifles and hiked up the ridge to have a look at the hunter's sheep. By the time they got there, the backslaps and handshakes were all over with. The hunter was sitting beside his ram, watching Mike as he approached. It took only seconds for Mike to take in the beauty of this great ram with his salt-and-pepper cape and perfectly symmetrical, wide-flaring thirty-nine inch horns. With an envious smile he reached out and shook the old hunter's hand.

"Congratulations," he said, "you got yourself a beautiful ram!" Then he turned to Kent and shook his hand. "Good work, Kent, that was an excellent stalk." Neil was in shock; this was the first sheep he'd ever seen.

Mike offered to take a few photos of them together with the ram, and then he took a few for himself. As Kent began skinning off the cape, Mike and Neil sat down and began a friendly conversation with the hunter. He was absolutely amazed that they were not upset with him for ruining their chance at the rams. He was also stunned at the size of packs they carried without batting an eye!

After the cape, horns, and meat were removed and loaded up, they headed back down to the saddle together. At the saddle, they said their farewells as Kent and his happy hunter headed for their horses down in the stunted balsams.

Mike and Neil hunted hard for a week, seeing plenty of rams every day. They were pounded unmercifully by fierce winds, rain and snow, which didn't help matters a whole lot. At one point Mike had a chance to try a three-hundred-yard steep downhill shot at a good thirty-nine inch ram. Darkness was approaching, he couldn't get a good rest and the wind was nearly hurricane force, so he declined.

Meanwhile, Chuck and I were pounding our sorry carcasses up the Stewart-Cassiar highway in my old Toyota. After stopping for lunch at a truck stop west of Watson Lake, I said, "Chuck, you'd better drive. I need to close my eyes for awhile." That was quite a thrill for him. He had just gotten his driver's license and here he was dodging trucks and tourists on the Alaska Highway.

About sundown, we arrived in Atlin, found a quiet campground and set up our little mountain tent. Chuck built us a nice fire while I cooked dinner. By the time it got black dark, we were finished eating and ready for bed. (In Northern BC, darkness, on the 6th of August, arrives at about midnight.)

Our flight was booked for mid-afternoon, so we slept in until 8:00 AM. I cooked breakfast while Chuck tore down camp and loaded everything back into the pick-up. After breakfast, we checked in with Summit Air Services, then drove out of town to a gravel pit to check the zero on my old .243. It was bang-on at 200 yards — perfect for sheep hunting.

As the day wore on, the wind picked up until, by the time it was our turn to fly, the lake was shore-to-shore whitecaps. A small island a few hundred yards off the beach broke the waves up enough so that float planes could still take off and land.

Chuck and I unloaded our gear and carried it all out to the float. I parked the pick-up and went in to the office to pay for the trip. Meanwhile Chuck noticed an older gentleman, who turned out to be from the U.S., sitting near the dock and struck up a conversation with him. He was impressed that Chuck was going on this hunt with his dad, and that he had been going on fly-in hunts since he was only six years old. He was also surprised to hear that Chuck was on the Stewart Volunteer Fire Department and was planning to become a journeyman in carpentry.

After the pilot fuelled the aircraft, a turbo 206 Cessna, we loaded up our gear and climbed in. We were more accustomed to riding in Super Cubs, Beavers and Otters, so we didn't quite know what to expect from this particular aircraft.

Much to my satisfaction, both plane and pilot performed admirably and we were soon pointed in the right direction. A heavy blanket of sinister-looking storm clouds forced the pilot to fly at a lower altitude through narrow mountain passes and around scattered snowstorms. We were tossed and jerked around quite violently at times, as we crossed rugged ridges and canyons.

About the time I was ready to re-cycle my breakfast, the pilot began to fiddle with the engine controls in preparation for landing. As he gently pushed the nose down and throttled back, the lake magically appeared from behind a nasty snow squall. This was my first trip to this lake and I must admit, a more desolate chunk of real estate would be hard to find. The whole place was standing on end. The steep slopes on both sides of the narrow lake were a mass of broken rock, narrow benches, and vertical cliffs. The ridge-tops and surrounding basins were covered in a rich bed of pale green tundra interspersed with jagged black lichen-covered boulders. It looked, for all the world, like sheep paradise to me.

Our pilot expertly manoeuvred the plane onto the water and we were fast taxiing toward the north end of the lake when I spotted our base camp on the eastern shore. A few hundred yards from camp he throttled right back and the plane settled into the water like a fat loon.

Mike and Neil came down to the shore and caught hold of the plane so the floats wouldn't be damaged on the rocks. The pilot jumped out and helped Mike to hold the floats while Chuck and I got to shore. Then we turned the plane around and pulled it tail-first up onto the soggy grass.

I turned to Mike and said, "You look like the last rose of summer!"

He said, "That's what I feel like too! You know, Dad, we didn't get a sheep but it doesn't matter — we had one hell of an adventure and we got to see lots of nice rams." Neil agreed wholeheartedly. Mike gave me a quick run-down of the situation as Chuck and Neil helped the pilot unload the plane.

We walked up to the camp and I said, "Why do you guys still have so much grub left over?"

He said, "We've been out in spike camp the whole time! We just got back to base camp last night!" We sorted through the food and I kept just enough to keep Chuck and I alive for a few days. We put the rest in the plane for the trip out. Mike pulled a bottle of Crown Royal out of a paper bag and said, "Here, Dad, if you and Chuck get a ram, have a drink on us."

We all shook hands and wished each other the best of luck, and they were off. As the plane flew out of sight behind the mountains, I couldn't help but feel sorry for Mike. This had been his fourth sheep hunt — his first carrying a rifle — and he still didn't have a ram. I thought to myself, "That's okay, Mike, you're only eighteen. When you finally get a ram, it's going to be a dandy!"

Chuck and I were both a little queasy from the flight, so we set up our tent and had a little snooze. Late in the afternoon, we cooked up a big meal, cleaned up the dishes and went to bed early.

We dragged out weary tails out of bed at 4:00 AM and had hot coffee, bread, honey and peanut butter while our sleeping bags were airing out. By 5:00 we were loaded up and pointed up the horse trail. During the night, the whole country had received a light blanket of snow, then the sky had cleared and 'Jack Frost' had taken over. The muddy trail was frozen solid, so we had good going for the first few hours. Although we stopped often to rest and glassed for sheep every time, we didn't see anything but a very lonely cow caribou.

At 2:00 PM, after nine hours on the trail, we arrived at the 'saddle' in a cold misty rain. We struggled out of our packs, grabbed our bino's and crawled to the rim of the saddle. What a treat this was! A high valley, originating in a wide grassy pass five miles to the north, ran down to a mile-wide basin below us, then fell off into a deep timbered canyon to the east.

It was difficult for us to see much of anything in the blowing mist, but we were determined to give it a shot. We had pretty much covered everything in sight, when I noticed movement directly below us in the basin. "Rams, Chuck! Right here below us!" We started counting ... fourteen rams. Some were up feeding and others were bedded down, all at about half a mile.

As excited as we were, we had to do the right thing — we set up camp. This took only a few minutes, so, no matter when we got home, our gear would be safe and dry.

A bench below and to our right seemed to run a long way out toward the rams before dropping off abruptly. It was hard to tell from our angle if we could get close enough but we were going to try. With our packs and rifles on, we cut back to the east and crossed the ridge out of sight. The first hundred yards of the north side was across a big snow patch. Then we broke out onto the tundra. At a little rocky outcrop we could go no further and were still six or eight hundred yards above them.

We got out the spotting scope and set it up. At least four of the rams were over full curl, with two of them un-broomed at close to 40 inches. As we sat watching them, I couldn't keep my eyes off the nearest one.

Both horns were broomed back and his whole front end was nearly pure white. He appeared to be nearing the end of the trail, as he was noticeably thin in comparison to the others. Suddenly, as if he felt my eyes on him, he stood up and walked deliberately down the hill about forty yards, then turned to the right and walked straight east along the base of the ridge.

Another ram, this one big and fat with a dark salt-and-pepper cape and heavy, slightly broomed horns, stood up and walked over to a big flat rock. He stepped up onto the rock and posed there like a statue as he watched the older ram walk out of sight around the ridge. He glanced back to the left at the others, who were now slowly feeding towards the north then, as if suddenly in a hurry, he jumped off the rock and trotted off after the old ram. Three young rams, the last ones still bedded, suddenly stood up, had a quick stretch and also trotted after the old guy. The nine remaining rams didn't even seem to notice that their friends had left. A low ridge of glacial moraine across the bottom end of the basin looked like a good place for an ambush as the remaining nine sheep were feeding about a hundred yards below it. Back up the slope to our left, a shallow draw ran down into the basin. Chuck and I scrambled back up the hill and, with the rams all feeding downhill and away, turned down the draw at a run. Near the bottom of the basin we checked on them with the bino's. They were still feeding, but moving farther away from the moraine ridge. We turned on the afterburners, practically running the last six hundred yards to the low ridge.

By the time we got there, the rams had fed out of sight into the creek bottom and were about four hundred yards away. As we sat contemplating our next move, I had the wild urge to cover the next two hundred yards at run then sit out in the open and wait for them to come back up out of creek.

There was no need to worry. Before we had a chance to come up with another plan, the lead rams were already feeding their way up the far side of the basin. They were then at five hundred yards and unless they changed direction, we would soon be out of luck. I set up the spotting scope and focussed on the two lead rams. They were, without a doubt, as picture-perfect as any two rams could be. One was nearly pure white, while his best friend was a very dark salt-and-pepper colour. Their horns appeared to measure about forty inches, and were at least five inches past full curl.

Our situation began to look impossible, with the rams moving farther away and higher up the side of the basin. They'd soon be able to look

115

right down on us, so we crawled in behind the tallest cover we could find — a little patch of two-foot high arctic willow. We continued glassing them until they finally bedded down in the rocks high on the northwest wall of the basin, a good thousand yards away. Now that they were not distracted by food, some of the rams began to notice that something was not quite right in their neighbourhood. The two big guys were the first to zero in on us, then the younger ones began to pay attention.

Late in the afternoon, the sun finally broke through the clouds and just in time, as the wind was beginning to blow straight down on us from an ice field in the rugged western corner of the basin. This only lasted for an hour before it disappeared over the mountain directly behind the rams. Finally, we had to make a move before we both ended up sick.

"Are you getting cold, Chuck?" I asked.

"Yeah, I am," he answered. "This wind is blowing through me like I don't have anything on!"

"Well," I said, "they know we're here, and it doesn't look like they're going to make the first move, so we may as well get back to camp and have dinner."

We got into our packs and walked straight up the south side of the basin toward camp. As soon as we stood up, the rams all jumped up and ran a short distance up the rugged slope, then stopped to watch us. We carried on up our side and they slowly worked their way up and over the northwest rim.

Back in spike camp, we had our supper, which consisted of dry Chinese noodle soup mix ('simply pour boiling water into it'), beef jerky, fruit leather and a chocolate-covered granola bar to top everything off. After that we brushed our teeth and headed for the sack. Our tent was sitting on an interesting spot. We couldn't find any level ground, so we parked it out on a large square rock, which was partly buried in the mountainside. As a consequence, a careless first step out the front door of the 'Chateau Ferguson' was guaranteed to create an invigorating experience.

Morning found us in a wind-blown, heavy mist, glassing the basin again as we munched on our cold breakfast (granola, trail mix, fruit leather, vitamin pills and water). It wasn't eggs benedict, but it did the trick.

There was not a single sheep in sight, so we decided to hunt the eastern end of the ridge we were camped on. It was only two miles to where the ridge dropped off into the timber, and that's the direction the skinny old white ram and his friends had gone. That was also the direction of the wind, but it was blowing so hard I was sure nothing would be able to pick up our scent. The mist, heavy at times, had us chilled to the bone, so we quickly got our gear together. By 5:00am, we had our packs on and were picking our way carefully along a very tricky sheep trail — tricky in that it wasn't really a trail. It was a four hundred-yard-wide jumble of broken, square-cornered boulders sitting precariously on the steep southern slope. Many of these boulders were ten to fifteen feet across and covered with black lichen. The only indication that sheep had traveled here at all was a faint one-foot-wide disturbance in the lichen across these rocks.

Fig 22:
"We set our tent on an "almost" flat spot"

We took our time hunting the ridge, stopping often to glass every new piece of rock and tundra. A few times, as we crossed low saddles on the ridge, we sat down and glassed the ridge two miles across the big basin to the north. At one point, the sun broke through and we instantly spotted a large band of ewes, lambs and young rams bedded on a broad slope. Although the heat waves made it difficult, we counted over thirty head in total.

Mid-afternoon found us at the south-eastern corner of the ridge, where it dropped straight off into a rugged canyon full of jagged boulders and twisted balsams. Several ghostly hoodoos of various heights and shapes stood like statues along the canyon's edge below us. They

117

were anywhere from twenty to sixty feet high and some had sheep beds on their flat, grassy tops.

We had noticed the strong smell of sheep several times during the day, but this place smelled and looked more like a barnyard, with fresh sheep sign all around. We peeked over every cliff and around every rock and found nothing. We had no choice but to make our way back to camp. We had glassed the entire north and south sides of the ridge on our way down, except for a little piece out on the northeast corner.

The end of the ridge was fairly flat, but resembled a moonscape with big boulders scattered all across the surface. Chuck and I carefully picked our way over and around them on our way to the north side. We were beginning to get hungry and the sunny periods were getting more frequent, so I was looking for a strategic place to rest. We found that special place out where the north-facing slope dropped out of sight into the valley. It was a grassy bowl out of the wind and facing into the sun. We got out of our packs, dug out the beef jerky, trail mix and water, and had lunch.

We were sitting back in the sun wondering what we had to do to find a ram, when it happened — I spotted movement.

"**S**heep!" I blurted as I grabbed my bino's. "Rams too!" We both grabbed our gear and dragged it into the bottom of the little basin. Then, with the spotting scope set up, we had a look. It was the old skinny ram and his band. They were over three hundred yards away along the ridge at our level and feeding uphill toward our left. The big dark coloured ram was in the lead with the three youngsters close behind. The old guy was about fifty yards back and a little farther away from us.

I told Chuck, "Hurry up! Get a rest set up!" I checked the .243 and passed it to him and said, "Take the big ram."

He wiggled into position and I asked, "How's it look?"

"It looks like a long way," he answered. I reached over and cranked the Leopold scope up to 12 power and he said, "That's better, but it's still a long way."

"Hold a foot over the top of his back," I told him. "Remember to just squeeze the trigger." I had settled in behind the spotting scope to watch his shot when he said, "Dad, I can't see him. That big rock is in the way." I looked and, sure enough, a big boulder in front of us was blocking his shot.

"Okay," I said, "can you see the old one below?"

"Yeah, I can see him okay," he said.

"Good," I said, "give him a try."

As soon as the ram stopped and put his head down to feed, Chuck let the shot go. I got the surprise of my life. Through the spotting scope, I saw the shock wave of the bullet as its path curved high above the ram, then dropped back down to connect. The ram turned away, walked a few steps, and tipped over.

"Okay!" I said. "Let me in there!" Chuck slid back out of the way and I crawled in behind the .243. The big ram, by this time, had turned around and was looking back down at the old guy. I quickly picked him up in the scope and, holding a foot above his back, squeezed the shot off. I lost sight of him with the recoil, but Chuck said he was down.

I reached over and shook his hand and said, "Good work, Chuck! You didn't get the biggest one, but you damn sure got the prettiest!" He took the rifle and walked toward his ram. The young rams, in the confusion, thought that the older rams were bedding down for the afternoon and had all bedded down in a group. I could imagine their surprise as Chuck walked up with the rifle in his hands.

I watched through the spotting scope while Chuck walked by my ram. The young rams jumped to their feet and stood thirty yards up the hill, leaderless, and not having the foggiest idea what to do about it. Meanwhile, Chuck was having trouble finding his ram among all the sheep-coloured rocks. He looked back at me with his bino's and I gave him hand signals, finally leading him to the old ram.

I looked at my watch; it was 5:00 PM. We had been on the trail for twelve hours and the hard work was about to begin. I gathered up our gear, put Chuck's pack on top of mine, and headed over for a look at our rams. I was impressed. My ram was as fat as a pig, with a most beautiful salt-and-pepper cape. His heavy horns were broomed back to 37 inches and came well above the nose.

I walked the hundred yards over to Chuck's ram, and there sat a happy kid. This old guy would very likely not have made the winter, given the condition of his teeth. His cape was nearly pure white, which is not uncommon for rams this far north. His horns were nicely broomed back and carried good weight right to the flared out tips. What a beautiful ram he was.

We got out the camera and tripod, took a bunch of photos and got down to work. I helped Chuck with the opening cuts on his ram, then went back and started on mine. An hour later, the cape was off and the meat was all boned out and cooling on meat bags. I walked over to see how Chuck was making out.

He wasn't doing too well. He had a splitting headache and was sick to his stomach. Having had allergic reactions in the past, I suspected he was reacting to the ram's hair. I sent him over to a small spring to wash his hands and face and have a drink. When he came back, I made him rest upwind of the ram while I finished up the knife work.

Fig 23:
"Chuck didn't get the biggest one, but he damn sure got the prettiest!"

By the time we got our heavy loads on and got moving, it was 8:00 PM. We had three hours to make it three miles back along the rugged trail before dark. It spite of his condition, Chuck didn't slow down. We put on a forced march up the ridge and, just as it got dark, we made it across the last of the boulder field.

About two hundred yards from camp the trail went up over a low ridge. That last little burst finished me off. I found a bench of rock to sit on where I could lean back against my pack. Chuck carried on down to camp carrying the .243 in case we had visitors of the hairy kind. I was content to sit and watch the final curtain come down over the Southern Yukon.

Chuck's voice sounded miles away. "Dad, do you want me to come up and get your pack?"

"No, its OK Chuck," I lied. "I'll be there in a few minutes."

I didn't know if I could get up on my feet again, but somehow I did. I made my way carefully down to the tent where Chuck grabbed my pack and helped me unload. It was 11:00 PM and suddenly very dark on the south side of the ridge — the end of an eighteen hour day. We pulled the meat bags and capes out of our packs, spread them out to cool, and had a little snack. I took three extra-strength Tylenol with water for dessert and fell into bed.

Fig 24:
"My ram had a most beautiful salt-and-pepper cape."

We both put our hearts into the fine art of snoring that night. On a scale of one to ten, we very likely scored a twelve.

In the morning, I woke up hot and thirsty. It was only 5:00am, but the sun was cooking us inside the tent. I sat up, unzipped the door and looked out. There was not a cloud in the sky. I climbed out, moved all the meat into the shade behind the tent, and had a look around. For the first time since we had arrived, I could see for a hundred miles, and it was beautiful. I cooked us up the meal we should have had the night before, and with our bellies full again, we kicked back onto the tundra for another snooze.

By 10:00am, the clouds were beginning to move in from the Gulf of Alaska, so we decided to pack up and head for base camp. We were soon on our way with loads that nearly took our breath away. At one of our rest breaks, we got out the camera and took a few photos. I said, "Chuck, you'd better take a picture of me packin' this sheep off the mountain, it may never happen again."

Late in the afternoon, after another forced march, we made it into base camp. I put both a kettle and a big pot of water on the propane stove to boil for our showers. Then we pulled all the meat bags out of our packs and hung them up with the capes. We hooked our solar shower bag to the end of a long pole which was balanced and tied over a balsam branch eight feet above the ground. With a six-foot length of rope, we pulled the other end down and tied it to the base of another tree, hoisting up the solar bag in the process.

After showering and changing into clean clothes, I cooked a big dinner of sheep fillets, potatoes, corn and beer. I don't think anyone in the free world enjoyed a meal as much as we did that night.

While I washed the dishes, Chuck gathered a pile of firewood and stored it in the 'den'. This was a flat, rocky area below the cook tent, protected from the wind by a semi-circle of twisted balsams. We pulled a few rocks out of the ground, forming a rough circle with them, and lit a big fire right in the middle. With the fire and a hot toddy, it seemed so much like home that we finished the décor by hanging our new sheep on the wall.

The next morning, after breakfast, we went to work on our capes, splitting the lips, turning the ears, and salting them down. With that chore out of the way we spent the rest of the day relaxing and nursing our still tender feet. We had dinner early in the evening and retired to the den, where Chuck had a friendly fire going. I poured a few Cuba Libres, we drank to Mike and Neil, and proceeded to keep the neighbours up all night.

When we finally got to bed around midnight, we were paid a visit by a particularly large and vicious marten. He seemed determined to destroy our camp as he crashed around in the kitchen, knocking over dishes and scattering food all over hell's half acre.

Suddenly, out of the tent leaps Mountain Man Ferg, by equal parts, extremely fearless and naked! He carries a flashlight in one hand and an axe in the other. A lively conflict ensues around the brush, with the marten cleverly outmanoeuvring his adversary, who in the heat of the chase, nearly tears off his undercarriage.

Fig 25:
"Mountain Man Ferg nearly tears off his undercarriage."

Fig 26:
"We were soon on our way with loads that nearly took our breath away."

I retreated to the relative safety of my sleeping bag and left the marten to ransack our camp for the rest of the night. I'd like to think that Chuck was proud of me, even if I came out second best with the marten.

We spent the next two days relaxing around camp and enjoying the scenery. The plane picked us up just in time, as another blustery storm was threatening to move in. Chuck and I had a lot of fun on that trip, highlighted by sore muscles, blistered feet and many laughs.

•••

11
Gettin' Walter's Goat...

Walter Kornylo had a burning desire to hunt a mountain goat. He had made a few futile attempts at getting close to one, but in the process had discovered that goat hunting was just a touch dangerous to his health.

My two sons, Mike and Chuck, were both tagged out with nice billies to their credit. I had also filled my tag with an early November billy. Walter had nothing but a perpetual 'sad dog' look on his face and the thought that he would never get a chance at a billy.

One morning over coffee with Walter, I had what I thought was a bright idea. It seemed I had the time and could use a little exercise before winter set in, so I drained my mouth of the last sip of coffee and stuck in my foot.

"Walter, what do you think about going out first thing in the morning?" I offered. "Maybe we can find you a billy not too far up the mountain."

"Sure," he said, "what will I need to bring?"

"Well," I answered, "all you'll need is a good pack frame, lunch, warm clothes, and two hundred feet of light nylon rope. Make sure your gun is lined up!"

In the morning before daylight we were on our way out of Stewart. It was heavily overcast and raining lightly as we entered the Bear Pass. The wind was picking up out of the west, so it didn't look too promising. Finally, by the time we reached Bear Glacier, we were in an all-out blizzard of swirling snow.

A little farther along, I pulled off the highway into a gravel pit. The gusting wind rocked my Toyota pickup as we poured coffee. A few degrees warmer and we would have been experiencing rain. The pass was covered in six inches of crusted snow, where the normal amount for that time of year was between two and five feet.

The snow eased off, surprisingly, and we got a look at the mountainside. A quick squint through the bino's turned up a few goats right off the bat. One appeared to be a billy on the move. Acting like an old white tail buck, he was following a nanny's tracks all over the side of the mountain. It was indeed rutting season, and this billy was serious about his job. In the short time we spent watching him, he traveled nearly half a mile to the south, then dropped down two or three hundred yards and traveled over a half mile back to the north.

Eventually, he found the lady of his dreams and they moved off together to a secluded, snow-covered ledge out of the wind.

"OK, Walter, they'll stay bedded for a while," I said. "Are you feeling mean?"

"Yep, I think so." he answered.

I drove up the highway to a spot closer to where we'd start up the mountain. An old Cat trail behind a thick patch of spruce would be a perfect place to park out of sight.

Soon we were on our way up the side of the mountain. There was just enough old snow to make the footing good. For goat hunting, I wear my heavy plastic Koflach boots. They give me extra stability, while keeping my feet warm and dry in the snow.

An hour of steady climbing brought us nearly to the crest of a rugged boulder-strewn bench. We stopped to rest before tackling the last steep pitch.

Walter took this opportunity to inform me that he was afraid of heights. I looked at him and he was a little off-colour and trembling slightly. Having been in his position myself over the years, I said, "That's all right, Walter. Don't look down and you'll be fine."

The weather had improved considerably, so I pulled out my camera and we snapped a few photos of each other. When we were rested and ready to make the final burst over the top, I said, "Okay, Walter, stay right behind me and put your feet where I put mine."

We were over the crest of the bench within ten minutes and pushing our way through deep powdered snow and stunted balsam. On breaking into the open on the south side, we sat down and glassed for the billy. At five hundred yards, he was difficult to spot with the wind blowing great clouds of drifting snow over the ridge and into his bedroom. We finally managed to spot him and his lovely bride through the swirling white veil. They were bedded, facing away from each other, on the edge of a high cliff.

I had a little time to get Walter calmed down, so I swung into 'idiot mode' to loosen him up. "Walter," I said as I held my hands out flat, fingers pointed straight down and elbows at my side, "can you do this?"

He looked at me like I'd gone right off my rocker. "What the hell is that?" He asked.

"Don't you know anything about hunting?" I asked. "This is the famous Sylvester-the-Cat-sneakin'-up-on-Granny's-canary pose! We've got to get across to that other patch of balsam thirty yards away and this is the only way to do it" By then he was doubled over laughing with tears in his eyes. "Now listen!" I exclaimed, "I'm gonna send you across first. I'll

Fig 27:
"The famous Sylvester-the-Cat-sneakin'-up-on-Granny's-canary pose…"

watch with the spotting scope and if they're not lookin' our way I'll say 'Go'. Now don't screw up! I don't want that billy sayin', 'Ooh! I tot I taw a goat hunter!' Now, you got that straight?"

At that point we were both laughing so hard we couldn't stand up. It was a good thing the wind was howling up there, otherwise there wouldn't have been a goat left in the country.

Once Walter had his colour back, we were ready for action. We managed to cross the opening undetected, and were soon hidden by another patch of balsam.

By the time we had run out of cover again, we were still over three hundred yards away with a strong crosswind. I lay my pack on a little hump and got Walter lying prone with his 7 mm Remington Magnum resting over it. "Okay Walter," I said, "lay your cross-hairs on him and tell me how you feel." He had a

Fig 28:
"Good shootin' partner. You just got yourself a dandy goat!"

look through the scope. After awhile he said that it looked good. "Can you see your heartbeat moving the crosshairs on him?" I ask.

"No, it looks real steady," he answered.

"Okay," I said, "now you've got to trust me. Lay your crosshairs right at the tip of his horns and squeeze off your shot."

He looked up at me. "Really?"

"That's right," I said, "this is a long shot and the wind is going to drift your bullet." I watched through the spotting scope as he started the squeeze. At the shot, the billy jumped to his feet and turned toward the nanny. "Good job, Walter!" I said. "There's a spot of blood on his ribs. You got both lungs."

Then the billy lay down still facing the nanny. "Hold one foot over the top of his rump and give him another one Walter," I said, "maybe we can get him to jump over the edge and land on that grassy slope below."

At the shot he stood up again, then fell and rolled over the edge. About sixty feet down he landed on a narrow bench, hanging up against a balsam shrub.

I turned to Walter and shook his hand. "Good shootin' partner. You just got yourself a dandy goat!"

Twenty minutes later we were standing by a patch of balsam in two feet of snow, looking straight up at the goat. I put Walter to work building a fire while I climbed up around the left side of the cliffs. Within half an hour, I was standing beside the billy. I wasted no time in tying the rope around his neck and kicking him off the edge. With two wraps around the balsam, I was able to let him down slowly.

I was soon out of rope, so I peeked over the edge. He had only twenty feet to drop; I let go. He landed with a thud and started a small avalanche as he slid towards Walter.

Working my way back off the cliff, I climbed down to the goat and dragged him the rest of the way down to Walter. He was grinning from ear to ear as he admired his billy. We quickly took a bunch of photos and got to work skinning him for a life-size mount.

On the way back down the steep mountainside, with a big load of meat and a life-sized cape, Walter was so happy he forgot to be scared. He delivered his billy to Britton's Taxidermy in Smithers where they did a fantastic life-size mount for him.

•••

12

"Incoming Moose!"

Four years after the hunt for Ida's monster moose, I was back at the same lake. This time my hunting partner was Jack, 'the Swamp Fox' Fillion, a good friend from Stewart. Jack had shot a few moose before but never a big one.

The BC-Yukon Beaver dropped us off fairly early in the morning so we had plenty of time to set up camp. A chill wind blowing from the west instilled in us the urge to set up camp quickly. Ominous dark clouds cast an evil shadow as they rolled over the Coast Mountains out of the Gulf of Alaska.

After camp was set up, we dressed for the occasion, grabbed a few snacks and headed up the old familiar trail through the timber.

I was anxious to stand once again on the site where Ida's big bull had fallen that memorable day. An hour later, we were there above timberline, standing on the exact spot. All that remained was a little patch of stringy-looking grass that always grows where a gut pile has been.

I went through the whole adventure with Jack from start to finish. What a strange feeling: it almost seemed as if it took place fifty years ago.

We glassed from this spot for a while, then crossed the end of the little pool and worked out way up to the edge of the big bench. I mused that Chuckie would like to be here now. There was a whole new supply of caribou antlers scattered across the mountainside.

Up on the bench at the base of the mountain the wind was unmerciful. We moved along to the eastern end of the bench until it fell off sharply to a lower bench. There we found a bit of cover. Before glassing, Jack pulled out his snowmobile suit and slid into it. I took out my down vest and put it on under my wool jacket.

We began glassing and immediately located a cow moose two miles to the east on a low, sparsely timbered ridge. Soon, we spotted another cow moving from behind a patch of balsam. This was a good sign, as bulls were gathering cows this time of year.

"Keep an eye on those cows, Jack." I said. "I'm sure there's a bull with them."

"There he is!" Jack said, "just to the right of the cows!"

Sure enough. Between two clumps of balsam we could see a big white antler palm. After awhile, the bull moved out into the open and we got a good look at him. I estimated his spread to be around fifty-two inches. He was two miles from camp over some fairly soggy-looking ground.

"Well, Jack," I said, "If we leave him alone and don't spook him, we may find him closer tomorrow." Jack agreed.

Suddenly, I spotted movement a half-mile below and across a wide willow-covered draw. It was a pack of six wolves led by a large black male. They were travelling toward the moose to our right, but seemed to be nervous about something. I suspected they had picked up our scent when they crossed our trail down below.

As we watched them through the spotting scope, we noticed the unique colours on some of them. Two were black, two were grey, one was nearly white, and one was dark grey with light grey circles around his eyes.

Jack laughed. "Look at the circles around that one's eyes. He looks like a raccoon!"

The lead wolf kept stopping and looking ahead as if expecting something. That's when we heard it — the long, mournful howl of a wolf. The lead wolf froze in his tracks. The rest of the pack quickly crowded together. Then, as a second howl drifted from the timber, the lead wolf trotted back past the pack. Without looking back, they all fell in line behind their leader. They'd obviously been caught in the act of encroaching on another pack's territory.

Part of the way across the willow bottom, they turned uphill and were travelling straight towards us. At about six hundred yards, turning toward our left, they disappeared behind the crest of the grassy bench below. Jack and I jumped up and ran down onto the bench and kept moving until we spotted them again. They were partway up the slope and angling away about two hundred yards to our left. They hadn't seen us yet, so we got down and lined them up.

"Ready, Jack?" I asked. Well, so much for the silence. We built a lead fence around them and all but one escaped: the leader. When we got down there we were surprised at how skinny this old gentleman was. His hide wasn't in very good shape, so after a few photos we caped him out for a head mount and salvaged his skull.

On the way back to camp, before entering the scattered balsam, we took one last look at the bull to the east. He hadn't moved and very likely didn't hear the shots in the howling wind.

Back in camp, we had a big dinner and got to bed early. It was too damn miserable to sit up and talk.

Sometime during the night, the weather cleared up and it got real cold. Unzipping the tent, I looked out into a world of white. Everything was covered in hoarfrost. I was soon dressed and out of the tent getting coffee on. There was not a cloud in the sky and the sun was just touching the mountain peaks fifteen miles to the north. By the time coffee was ready, Jack was dragging his sorry carcass out of the tent. Now I know why he's a bachelor: he ain't real pretty in the morning!

As I stood there pouring us a coffee, I said, "Jack, have a look across the lake. There should be a moose standing over there somewhere." He lifted his bino's and had a long sweeping look across the frost-covered miles of arctic birch and stunted willow.

"Nope, I don't see anything," he answered. As I mixed in the sugar and cream, I peeked over the edge of our cover tarp. "What do you mean, Jack? I can see moose from here without bino's!" I exclaimed.

With a coffee in each hand, I walked over to Jack. A short balsam by the lakeshore was in his line of sight. "Move over two feet, Jack, and look again," I said.

"Well! Dog bite my ass!" He said, "there's two bulls and a cow!"

I wasted no time in setting up the tripod and spotting scope. At just under a mile, they showed up quite well on twenty power. A young cow, about to fall in love for the first time in her life, was running around the two bulls in crazy circles, tossing her head all the while. I could only imagine the wild vocalizations she was making.

The young bull, obviously confused by her crazy antics, stood alertly watching her every move. The larger bull, carrying what I guessed to be about a forty-inch rack, appeared to be tired of her foolishness.

As the first brilliant rays of sun fell on them, I zoomed the scope up to forty-five power and re-focussed. Amazingly, even at that range, I could see the big bull's right eye sparkle in the sun as he faced northeast. The moderate breeze was blowing from the south behind us. If I gave a cow call, he would pick it up quite easily, as he was almost directly downwind.

"Keep an eye on him, Jack," I said. "I'm going to lay a 'desperately-in-love' cow call on him."

It was easy to tell when the call reached him, as he turned his head to the right and looked directly at us. After a bit he looked away again, thinking, I guess, that he was only imagining things.

Then I laid another love song on him. That did it. He wasn't hearing things after all, and he had serious business to take care of. He headed for the north end of the lake to our right. We couldn't hear him, but his mouth opened every few seconds as he grunted his way along.

"Well Jack, get ready!" I said. "It looks like breakfast will have to wait."

"Ferguson," he answered, "how am I to keep my athletic figure if I don't eat?!" We both chuckled under our breath and grabbed another cup of coffee.

Thirty yards north of camp was a grassy creek bottom two hundred yards wide. It ran southeast from the lakeshore clear up to timberline. And thirty yards from the beach was a low grassy hump, possibly the remnants of an old beaver lodge. This would be a perfect spot to set up our ambush.

Sitting in the sun, partly hidden by the tall grass, we were ready for action. Every time the bull stopped, I gave him another call. He soon rounded the northeast corner of the lake and was now moving toward us. He went out of sight in a low spot and I stopped calling.

A wide buffer of arctic birch and stunted willow separated the lake from a long strip of scrubby balsam. For twenty minutes Jack and I sat there quietly enjoying the sun and solitude. Then, ever so faintly, a sound drifted from the timber above.

"Jack!" I said. "Do you hear that?" Confused, he looked up toward the top left edge of the willow bottom.

"It's a moose," he said, "and he's coming from way up there!" Before long, the calls became very distinct. We hadn't expected the bull to show up that soon.

Suddenly, out of the balsam five hundred yards above, strode a big bull moose. Not the one from across the lake, but the one we had seen with the two cows up at timberline. He must have been able to hear the other bull coming, because he was not wasting any time. Grunting constantly, he was headed straight for our tent, which, fortunately, was hidden behind a thick wall of balsam.

Jack and I lay side by side on the crest of the grassy hump with our heads up just enough to watch the bull's progress. If he stayed on the same course, he'd cross thirty yards in front of us.

In the meantime, the bull from across the lake materialized from the balsam about four hundred yards above us. With the big bull closing within a hundred yards of us, the smaller bull decided to try and beat him to the cow. He started off running across the willow bottom toward the timber on our right.

By that time, the big bull was at thirty yards and still grunting. I touched Jack's arm and, almost in one motion, he sat up and delivered a shot to the lungs. Then, for good measure, he cranked another round in and shot him through the antlers.

Fig 29:
Jack and his bull only 100 yards from camp.

The bull up the hill was nearly forgotten in the fray. He had spun around and was headed back toward the thick timber. At three hundred yards, I held six inches below the hump and fired. Then, just for insurance, Jack and I both repeated step one. The bull ran behind a patch of balsam but didn't come out the other side.

"He flinched on that first shot, Pat," said Jack, "and he didn't come out the other side. Maybe we should leave him for awhile."

"Good idea," I responded. "We're going to be tired boys tonight Jack. Congratulations, you shot a dandy moose!"

We dressed the big bull after we took a few photos, then headed up to see about the other one. Just then a raven flew over in the general direction where the second bull had disappeared. "Watch that raven, Jack!" I said. "He'll tell us where the bull is."

The very second he reached the balsam patch he turned sharply and flew a few tight circles. "Yep, he's still there," I said, "let's go."

When we got closer, we split up and moved in. Jack found him first and put one in his neck, just for safety's sake. We took a few more photos and got down to work.

134

Fig 30:
"We took a few photos and got to work."

By the end of the day, we were tired and hungry, but the mountain of meat stacked by the lake made it all worthwhile. Thankfully, I had asked for the Otter to pick us up, as the Beaver would have had to come back for a second load.

The only disturbing thing about this trip was the dramatic increase in the wolf population since Ida's trip four years earlier. We had seen wolves every day, and lots of cow moose without calves.

•••

13
Caribou in Paradise...

The year 1987 hadn't exactly been kind to me, financially. All of the mining operations in the Stewart area had shut down because of low copper and gold prices, and the logging companies weren't doing much better. I had taken advantage of the typically gorgeous north coast spring weather to hunt a few black bears with the kids and get our firewood in for the coming winter. Summer came and left without a trace of work anywhere on the horizon. That left me plenty of time to take the slack out of our deep freeze with a few king salmon.

When early September rolled around, I got lucky and caught a young bull moose with his pants down, so our freezer was once again full to the lid. What a great feeling!

That was when I received the phone call — it was Gene Allan from the Kispiox Valley.

"Hi, Fergie! How's it going?"

I chuckled and said, "It's not going worth a damn but I appreciate your concern. What the hell do you want? Don't you realize I can get jail time just for talkin' to you?"

There was a big laugh on the other end. "I'm just callin' to make you a hell of a deal!"

I said, "That's exactly why I've got goose bumps — the last thing I need is one of your 'helluva deals!'"

Another big laugh. "No, nothin' dangerous, I just wanted to see if you were interested in guidin' hunters for Ron Fleming. I was supposed to fly in tomorrow, but I blew out my knee doggin' steers at the Smithers Rodeo."

"Tomorrow!" I said. "Jesus, you sure give a guy lots of warning!" I thought about it for a second or two. Well, it was work, so I got with the program and threw a little gear together. Besides, I was booked for my third back operation in early December, so this would give me a chance to be in peak condition for a quick recovery.

At four o'clock the next morning I gave Ida one last kiss and hit the trail. Four hours later I was sitting on the dock at Tyhee Lake outside of Smithers waiting for the de Havilland Beaver to pick me up.

There was not a soul in sight, and the only sign that someone may show up anytime soon was a Cessna 185 tied up to the dock. In a few minutes the owner showed up with a big load of gear and groceries, so I helped him carry it down to the plane.

After a short conversation I discovered that his name was Keith Connors. He had a guiding territory on the Finlay River, just east of where I would be guiding. It took only a short flurry of action before he was loaded and on his way.

An hour later, the Beaver landed and drifted quietly up to the dock. When the young pilot stepped out onto the float, I introduced myself and we proceeded to load the plane — and 'load' we did. First, he removed the front passenger seat and we slid in several sheets of roofing in. Next, we wrestled two 45 gallon drums of gasoline up a crude ramp and through the cargo door. Then came several bags of oats and a few large cardboard boxes of groceries.

With a look of smug satisfaction he turned to me and said, "Well, jump in!"

My jaw fell open. "Jump in where?" I said. "You were loaded before you put the oats in!" He looked at me as if I were crazy.

"I left room for you behind the gas drums," he told me. I looked through the small side window and, sure enough, he had left me a space just under two feet wide between the upright gas drums and the rear bulkhead. Wonderful. I looked down at the floats and they were nearly under the water on the back end. I looked across the lake, and there was not a breath of wind over the water.

"How the hell are you going to get this thing off the water?" I asked. "It's too warm and calm for a load like this!"

He smiled at me with a look of arrogant confidence and said, "Don't worry, we'll get off okay." I wasn't convinced, but in a moment of pure insanity I grabbed my gear and climbed over the mountain of supplies and weaseled my way in behind the gas drums which, by now, had filled the cabin with fumes.

Just for good measure, he stuffed two more big boxes of groceries up into the remaining space against the ceiling. With my duffel bag for a seat, I sat back to enjoy a "once in a lifetime" adventure.

He idled the plane up to the north end of the lake and turned in the reeds. Halfway through his turn, he began to open up the throttle and by the time the plane was pointed straight down the lake he was at full throttle. The lake was just over two miles long, and by the time we reached the other end we were still not even close to flying. He shut her down and idled around the south end for awhile, giving the engine a chance to cool down. If nothing else he at least caused some wave action and used up a bit of fuel.

After a few minutes he gave it another try and the waves from the first attempt helped to bounce us free of the water. At the north end of the lake we were only two hundred feet above the timber with the throttle still nearly wide open, but we were climbing slowly. Twenty miles out he backed the flaps off one notch and it felt like we were losing altitude, but it soon felt a little better as our speed picked up and we burned off more fuel.

Slowly, I began to relax and enjoy the ride in spite of the gas fumes and my cramped quarters. As we flew north toward Ron's area, I tried spotting game out the small rear window of the Beaver and was surprised to see a life and death drama unfolding beneath our right wing.

A black bear sow with two yearling cubs in tow was pulling a sneak on a small herd of nanny goats with kids. She was working her way down the shoulder of a tundra covered ridge directly above the goats, who were feeding on a series of steep benches a few hundred feet below. I could picture her mouth watering as she took in the delicious musky smell of the goats, one of the bears' favourite treats.

The ridge drifted slowly behind us, leaving them to their daily quest for food and happiness. As we flew north, the tundra covered mountains of the Babine Range gave way to the wide timbered valleys of the Sustut River and its many tributaries. The Sustut joins forces with, among others, the Babine and Bulkley Rivers to form the mighty Skeena River, one of the greatest salmon-producing rivers in North America.

To the north of this great river system, the tundra covered mountains and plateaus of the Tatlatui Park came into view, and they were breathtaking. We were flying low enough to see the many game trails quite well, as they crossed the open talus slopes. Oddly, I noticed a lack of fresh tracks on these trails, which should have shown up quite easily from the air, as these types of slopes show fresh tracks readily.

Before long, the pilot began his landing approach by throttling back and pumping on a few more degrees of flaps. Just before we touched down on the water the camp flashed by my little side window. It certainly appeared to be well established, with a large building out on the point and a few smaller log cabins back toward the timber. This is the base camp of Love Brothers and Lee, owned and operated by Ron Fleming and Brenda Nelson.

Brenda and her six year old son, Silas, met us on the dock with a hearty northern welcome while their dog, a border collie cross, made a grab for my hind leg. I threw him my very best move and came away unscathed in spite of his determined effort. In that fleeting instant I made a mental note to be sure and run a slug through him at the first opportune moment.

I was feeling a little sick to my stomach from all the gasoline fumes so after snapping a photo of the camp with the Beaver taking off in the background, I went to my cabin for a little snooze.

Sometime late in the afternoon, I was awakened by the sound of an outboard motor approaching out on the lake. I walked out the door just as Ron pulled up to the dock with his hunter. He stepped out onto the dock with a big grin on his face and shook my hand. "Howdy, Ferg!" He said, "thanks for comin' out — we're goin' to be up against it here for a couple of weeks."

Then he turned and introduced me to George Shore, a big bull of a man with a firm handshake. We tied the boat up for the night and headed for the main lodge.

Little did I know I was in for such a pleasant surprise. Having been around a lot of hunting camps, I was accustomed to the usual fine dining — meat, potatoes or rice, and canned vegetables.

Brenda has this nasty little habit of cooking two main courses every single night, with two types of salad and several desserts. As we enjoyed our meal, I began to wonder why Ron didn't weigh six hundred pounds. Then I came up with a few conclusions — he's got worms, a hollow leg, or he goes for liposuction every two weeks (I didn't bring that up at the table.).

After supper, with the slack out of our pelts and coffee in our hands, we retired to the living room where Ron kept us entertained for the rest of the evening. All the while little Silas, who very closely resembles Dennis the Menace with his blonde hair and energy level, never strayed too far away and kept looking up at me. Obviously he had overheard his dad talking to somebody about me coming to guide for them.

"Fergie?" He said, very quietly.

"Yes, Silas?" I answered.

"Do you really have eyes like an eagle?" He asked, as he stared directly into my eyes.

I chuckled quietly and, with my hand on his little shoulder said, "Well, Silas, I guess I do have fairly sharp eyes. Do you think my eyes look like eagle eyes?"

"I don't know," he said, "I never got to look at an eagle's eyes yet."

"Well," I said, "when you do will you let me know what they look like?"

He smiled and said, "Okay, Fergie," and drifted off to do his homework.

The next day Don Hartle, my first hunter, arrived on the plane. He was a professional fireman from the city of Las Vegas and, like most people in his line of work, appeared to be in peak condition. We spent the afternoon getting acquainted and checking out his rifles at the range. He had two beautiful custom-built rifles, one in .300 Winchester magnum and the other in .338 Winchester magnum. They both had an off-set, thumbhole stock.

Don and I spent the next few days hunting the many high drainages running into the main valley. We saw a few caribou everywhere we went, but nothing in the trophy category.

One evening, while sitting in the lodge, I said, "Ron, I can't help but notice the prominent game trails all over the country. Why so many heavy trails and so few fresh tracks on them?"

"Well, Fergie," he said, "a few years back the wolf population got completely out of control and nearly wiped out our caribou and moose. Then, with a big wolf population and low moose and caribou numbers, they started into the goats and sheep and pretty much wiped them out as well. Now, since they ate themselves right out of food, the wolf population has dropped off a bit and the game is beginning to recover slowly."

That night, Ron came up with a plan for Don and I, and the next morning we were off on a different kind of adventure. We were off to Brenda's fish camp down the famous Firesteel River, where we would base out of for a few days. Brenda packed us a big lunch and we loaded our packs for a week on the trail.

With fairly heavy packs on, we headed down the old horse trail that follows the river for several miles. Along the way, we stopped to admire waterfalls and trout pools of a kind that we thought only existed on calendars. The jack pine and balsam timber was short and thick in some areas but spotty in others with grassy, park-like meadows wandering everywhere. Entering one of these meadows we surprised a young caribou bull who had been lying down behind a patch of ten-foot-high balsams. He bolted out into the open meadow, then wheeled around to face us with his head held high and his eyes nearly popping out of his head. This was the most excitement he'd had in ages, as he pondered the thought of being eaten alive by these two wild looking creatures.

The early morning sun had just come from behind a fog bank, and was back-lighting the hair on his ears and the clouds of steam blowing from his flared nostrils. The testosterone-enhanced muscles on his neck looked over-inflated as they bulged out all the way from his shoulder to his jawbone. Most noticeable, though, was the peculiar cow-like nose, covered in silver hair. What a spectacular sight he was in the sparkling sunlight! Don and I stayed glued in our tracks until he finally let out a snort, reared up on his hind legs and trotted away in that peculiar mile eating gait.

By mid-day, we had passed above all of the steep canyons and found the little twelve foot aluminum boat and seven horsepower motor that Ron had left on a grassy hump. We slid the boat into the river, clamped on the motor and, with one pull of the starting cord, were riding down the river in style. That was quite a relief, as we were both nearly played out and ready for a rest.

With the little Mercury outboard idling along quietly, we covered the next few miles without producing a single drop of sweat. When we rounded the last bend in the river and spotted the lodge, it was easy to see why people came from all over the world to spend time at Brenda's Fish Camp. This place was a rare jewel set into the most incredible mountain scenery — and great trout fishing to boot.

We dragged the boat up onto the edge of a grassy meadow and walked over to check out the log cabin. The were plenty of beds in the back room and a large kitchen and dining room out front.

Don spent the rest of the day relaxing and glassing the surrounding mountains and tundra covered ridges for caribou, while I packed in two pails of water and got a few things ready for dinner.

Late in the afternoon, Don went up the river a few hundred yards and caught a pair of fat rainbow for supper, and what a feast we had! Their meat is red beyond belief, much like a sockeye salmon, and incredibly tasty. After our fine meal, we washed the dishes and sat down for a relaxing cup of coffee and a game of cribbage before drifting off to the sack.

Morning found us all rested up and ready for action. Ron had told me about a good place to hunt just down the river, so we threw our light packs into the boat and were on our way.

The first set of rapids really got our attention, but we made it through with minimal excitement, and were soon pulling the boat ashore at the trailhead. Across a wide grassy meadow at the base of a balsam and jack pine covered slope, we located the old horse trail. Although it hadn't seen any horse traffic in several years, it had been used by a few moose, caribou and bears, judging by the tracks.

The day had started out partly cloudy with intermittent warm sunny periods, but, as we approached the edge of timberline, the clouds began to show signs of rain or even snow. By the time we had climbed the last steep pitch of trail and stepped out onto the tundra, the wind had picked up dramatically. I looked at my partner and said, "Well, Don, what do you think?"

He just grinned. "It looks like we may have an interesting day." What a treat to have a hunter like him. He had suitable clothing and gear for this type of hunt as well as a positive attitude. He was destined to have a good hunt, no matter what happened.

Off to the west a dirty black storm was closing in on us fast, and, no matter which way we turned, we were going to be in it. "Well, Don," I said, "there's not much chance of finding any caribou on this side of the mountain. They'll all be on the far slope out of the wind. It's about two miles to the top of this long ridge, so, hopefully, by the time we reach the top, the storm will have blown past."

"Hell," he said, "I'm game. Let's do it."

We made it about a half a mile up the open ridge before the storm hit. Fortunately it was snow and not rain (rain gets you wet). The hiking was strangely easier with the wind practically blowing us up the ridge all the while plastering our backs with heavy wet snow. Visibility was down to about fifty feet, but we managed to stay on the very peak of the ridge. The storm, at one point, was so thick that it was nearly as dark as night, but we kept moving just fast enough to keep our body temperatures up. Then, out of the swirling snow, a little cluster of pumpkin-sized boulders took form. We were at the very summit of the mountain.

With nothing to see and nowhere to go I quickly got out of my pack and pulled out a ten-foot-square sheet of clear plastic. We brushed the snow off of each other, then, with our backs to the storm, sat on one end of the plastic and pulled the rest up over our heads. As the wind howled all around us I promptly fell asleep.

I awoke to Don bumping me and announcing the end of the storm. I was stiff and sore from my awkward sleeping position, but Don was ready for action. I shook the snow off the plastic sheet, folded it up and put it back in my pack. It was still snowing lightly, but the sun was beginning to break through, bringing its welcome warmth. The wind was still howling and brought tears to our eyes as we began glassing for caribou.

Now we had another problem. The whole country for miles around was covered in two inches of fresh, sticky snow, as were the caribou. We would have a tough time spotting them unless they were very close or on their feet and moving around.

Soon Don said, "I see a caribou!" I glanced over at him. He was looking at the far side of the big basin to our south. I had a quick look with my bino's and soon found a few more on the same mountainside. I set up the spotting scope and we had a better look at them on twenty power. There were a half dozen cows and a young bull. As Don studied them, I carried on glassing the rest of the country.

Fig 31:
Pat Ferguson (sitting) and Don Hartle with Don's bull caribou.

Suddenly my heart jumped into my throat. "Don, I think we just found your bull! He's right here below us about a half a mile away … there where the meadow starts."

Don picked the bull up in the spotting scope and said, "Man, he's sure nice and wide! He's got about eight or ten cows with him." I had a look through the scope at his impressive headgear.

"Well, Don, he's got long heavy, wide beams and his cape is beautiful. Look at that long white mane … I can't see his shovel or if he even has one."

We loaded up our gear and made our way down for a closer look. They had all stood up and shaken off the snow after the storm, but with the warm sunshine, had all bedded down again. We found a shallow gully to follow part-way down the mountain until we could line up a patch of balsam between us and the herd. In this way, we closed the distance to less than three hundred yards. I set up the spotting scope again and we studied the bull a little better. At this point we determined that he did not have a shovel, but had a long flat spike instead. Don still considered the bull a fine specimen, so we moved in closer for the shot. At one point, we were less than a hundred yards from him in the scattered balsam and wandering meadows, but the angle was wrong for a clean shot. We backed off.

At just over a hundred yards, Don finally had a clean shot. He crawled up behind a lone balsam, eased his .338 into position, and settled in behind it. When all was ready, he looked back at me and I gave him the thumbs-up. He turned, slid the safety off and started to squeeze.

The big bull's antlers fell to the side at the shot and all of the cows and calves jumped to their feet. A big cow ran over past the bull to our left, snorted a few times, then turned and ran back through the herd and up the mountainside leading the rest of the herd in her wake. She hadn't seen us, but our scent told her all she needed to know.

I walked over to Don and shook his hand. "Good work, Don," I said. "You got yourself a nice bull."

By this time, the wet snow down near timberline had all melted. We took our time examining the bull from one end to the other, and then set up the camera and tripod for a few photos. Next came the removal of the cape, a time consuming job under any conditions. Once the cape was safely out of the way, we skinned the rest of the animal and boned out the meat. After a little rest and a bite to eat, we loaded the meat into meat bags and into our packs. Next we bagged the cape and lashed the antlers onto Don's pack — the fun was over.

Though it was still early afternoon, we had a two mile uphill push ahead of us. It seemed endless at times, but with encouragement from each other and a little intestinal fortitude, we made it over the summit. Hiking down the horse trail fully loaded was pure hell on our knees. Still, somehow, by late afternoon we arrived at the river.

Don was a little apprehensive about riding the little boat back up the rapids. I ferried him across the river to a calm spot and began the charge myself. I thought I was setting a hot pace as I worked the craft in and around the tossing water, until I caught sight out of the corner of my eye of a movement on the bank. It was Don and he was lapping me, strolling along on foot.

Spurred by my injured pride, I regrouped, organizing the load closer to the stern, and gave it another try. This time, with the bow farther out of the water, I skimmed up the river as if I knew just what I was doing.

We treated ourselves to 'filet de caribou' that night and fell into the sack early. As I dozed off, I wondered how Ron and George were making out on the mountain behind camp hunting for caribou.

Next day we were treated to a typical mid-September morning for this country: bright sun and a vista of snow capped peaks. We wasted little time getting breakfast done so that we could start work on Don's caribou cape. Because he wanted to do all the work himself, I showed him how to split the lips and turn the ears in order that the salt, when applied, would penetrate the entire skin. While he worked, I cleaned up the cabin and got lunch ready.

Ron and George came steaming down the horse trail behind camp about mid-afternoon. They were all smiles and with reason, as George had scored on a beautiful big bull. Before supper that night, we had both capes fleshed, salted and ready for the taxidermist. We had another feast and celebrated our success with a few drinks from a bottle that Ron magically produced from his shirt.

In the morning, with the meat and capes hung out of reach of the bears, we all headed back up the river toward base camp. It was a long grind but that night we were treated to yet another of Brenda's 'magnum' meals. We also had a few new faces at the table that night. The Beaver had arrived with a new hunter and his lovely lady. He was looking for a nice caribou to take home to Los Angeles where he served a member of the S.W.A.T. team. We had no reservations about his ability with firearms. Also on the plane that day was Ron and Brenda's pretty, four year old daughter, Rena.

Perhaps the most interesting arrival on the plane was a distinguished gentleman named Ben DuBeau. Ben, who would be one of our guides for the rest of the season, was a man of some renown in the Hazelton-Kispiox area. He was a bachelor most of the time, but being a connoisseur of wild women and cheap beer, he did manage to lure the occasional prospective cook in the direction of his shack (more like his windbreak).

Ben struck quite a pose in his black cowboy hat and rustic western clothes. He was the hometown hero every year at the Kispiox Rodeo, where he was always entered in the saddle bronc' riding competition. Sometimes Ben went home with a small share of the prize money, but for the most part, after the wild cheering, bucking, squealing and farting was finished, he would limp out of the dusty arena quite happy in knowing that he'd entertained his many friends just one more time.

It was Don's last night in camp, so we all sat around and had one last good visit with him before drifting off to bed.

About mid-morning the next day, the Beaver showed up with my next caribou hunter, one Mr Phil Morton from southern California. We hurriedly off-loaded Phil's gear from the plane and loaded Don's in, sending him happily on his way. Don would return every year to hunt with Ron and Brenda, more, I suspect, for the food than for the exercise.

I got Phil and his gear settled into his cabin, and after checking his rifle at the range he came with me for a little stroll around the back side of the mountain near camp. He had a moose tag but was looking primarily for a caribou. Two miles of easy hiking along an old horse trail brought us to a low, bunch grass-covered ridge overlooking about eight hundred acres of small lakes and swamp meadows, topped off with scattered clumps of jack pine and balsam. This was moose paradise if I ever saw it.

I tried calling a few times and then we sat back in the sun and quietly talked the afternoon away. I've found that its always good to get to know my hunters before we get down to serious business. That night we had a little pow-wow after dinner to decide where everyone was going to hunt the next day. Ron suggested that I take Phil up to a camp at a higher lake for a few days and hunt caribou. I thought that this was an excellent idea, since I was gaining weight hanging around base camp and Brenda's plentiful cooking.

Just after daylight in the morning, Phil and I eased quietly away from the dock in one of Ron's freight boats, a twenty foot long wooden craft powered by a thirty-five horse outboard. We covered the length of the lake quickly, stopping once to add some clothing.

We located the valley where we were going to hunt and landed on a sandy beach. I searched around the edge of a bunchgrass meadow for a few green balsam sticks to place under the boat. This made it easier for us to slide the heavy craft up out of the water. Next, I cut a balsam stake and, after pounding it into the ground, tied the boat to it.

We shouldered our heavy packs and headed north up the valley. We soon found the horse trail that wound along a grassy bench on the eastern slope giving us a view of the country. The first few miles went well, with scattered clouds and a strong tail wind helping us keep cool as we hiked. Then a sudden gust of wind caught my attention and I turned to look into the teeth of a filthy black storm.

"Well, Phil," I said, "We've got to find some shelter for a while, so let's pick up the pace." There was no timber to speak of except for the odd twisted jack pine or balsam amongst the bunch grass and tundra, so we pressed on. About a half mile ahead, I saw the tops of what looked like a few big balsams behind a low ridge. Some sort of shelter.

Part way there the storm hit us with a vengeance and within minutes we were both plastered with heavy, wet snow.

"How are you doing, Phil?"

"I don't know Fergie," he answered, "I'm starting to get a chill."

"OK," I said, "One more good burst and we'll have a fire going behind that big balsam up ahead. Let's go!"

By the time I reached the tree, I was getting cold too, so I threw down my pack and, with my hatchet, chopped out a place for us to sit on the downwind side of the tree. I got Phil seated with his back to the tree and built a little fire in front of him.

"Just keep breaking up these dried branches and adding them to the fire. I'm going down to the creek to get some water in my 'billy can' so we can have a cup of hot tea."

Phil was warm and looking much restored when I returned with the water. I cut a four foot balsam stake, sharpened the big end, and pounded it into the ground at an angle with the top end directly over the fire. I hung the can by its wire handle from the end of the stick so that the bottom of the can was resting just in the fire. Next, I cut a pair of forked green willow sticks for sandwich toasters and gave one to Phil. We were soon eating toasted ham and cheese sandwiches, drinking hot tea and having a few good laughs with the snow swirling wildly around us.

Phil said with a grin, "You know, Fergie, this is the best hunting trip I've ever been on in my life. Does it get any better than this?"

I answered, "I guess it's all relative to what you expect out of the hunt, but you can be damned sure of one thing ... this adventure is a long way from over!"

Two hours and six inches of fresh snow later the end of the storm was in sight. We had just an hour of daylight left to cross the creek and find our cabin. Having arrived at the big balsam in the middle of the blinding storm, I had no idea exactly where we were relative to the camp. As a result, I was a good deal surprised as the lake slowly took shape only a few hundred yards to the north. The camp was supposed to be out on a wide grassy meadow halfway down the left side of the lake. We swung into action.

A quick walk up to the lake and back down to our tree didn't reveal the knee-deep crossing that Ron had told me about, so without wasting any more time I began peeling off the laundry. Phil's eyeballs nearly popped out of his head.

"You're getting naked in this weather?"

"You got any better ideas?" I said as I shoved my boots and clothes into my pack. "Stand right here on this hump and I'll be back to carry you across."

Ron had been partly right. The first twenty feet of the crossing was up to my knees, but the water was so cold it made my teeth ache. With fifteen feet to go I soldiered on right up to my belly button, which was about to pop off along with my severely diminished undercarriage. I swung my pack down on the bank and hurried back across.

"**C**'mon, Phil, jump on quick. I can't feel my legs anymore!" He hopped on and away we went. "Push down on my shoulders or your trailer hitch is gonna get wet."

He laughed and said, "You are one crazy bastard, Fergie!"

With Phil once again on dry land I rushed back to get his pack. As I came back across, (my fifth cruise) I said, "As soon as you get your pack on, get going and find the trail into camp. I'll catch up to you as soon as I get dressed." He didn't ask any questions, but shouldered his pack and lined out. I quickly got dressed, thankful that my feet were numb, as they were bleeding in several places. Finally, with my clothes and pack back on, I set out at a quick pace, following Phil's tracks through the chest-high arctic birch and stunted willow. I caught up to him at a low ridge of jumbled, truck sized boulders that looked as if they had been dumped out of a giant gravel truck a few decades before.

I stood beside Phil looking at this strange formation that ran from the lake on our right all the way to the base of the mountain three hundred yards to our left. Across the lake, on the mountainside to the east, was the answer to this mystery. A huge wedge of the mountainside had broken loose and shot down clear across the end of the lake without even blocking the river off.

It was too late to find a good trail, so we climbed up and over the rocky mess and were soon in sight of our new home. Several hundred yards away stood two lonely cabins out on the middle of a bunch-grass covered flat. Down on the lakeshore, I could make out a small aluminum boat upside down on the grass.

The valley appeared to have a little bit of everything to offer the hunter. To the west and north stood a series of jagged, snow plastered peaks and rugged slopes with 'mountain goat' written all over them. An interconnecting series of smaller lakes, wandering meadows and balsam patches ran from the north end of the lake. Across the lake to the east

Fig 32:
"Push down on my shoulders or your trailer hitch is gonna get wet."

stood a mountain that would cause any self-respecting caribou hunter's mouth to water. But for a thin strip of timber along the base of the mountain, its steep rolling slopes were covered in pure, clean tundra. This was caribou country at its best, and what was more, it ran for several miles to the south.

I had a good feeling about the morning as we marched into camp under the falling curtain of darkness. We were not long in swinging into action once inside the large, plywood and two-by-four, framed cook shack. I sent Phil down to the lake for a pail of water and then lit the wood stove with a handy pile of dry kindling and firewood. By the time he returned, the stove pipe was red hot three lengths up. I looked around at the set-up and discovered that Ron had the place hooked up with propane lights and a little cook stove. I soon had the lights on and dinner on its way.

This particular night we were treated to 'real man's food', that is, beans, corn, instant rice and square steak. Square steak, for the uninitiated, is canned Spork, sliced and fried. Phil choked and gagged a little, a sign that he was probably over-anxious to dive into this northern culinary delight. I took this reaction as an enthusiastic compliment from a man who, having lived most of his life on the California coast, had never really had the chance to challenge his pampered palate. In any event, the beans and corn kept our sleeping bags fluffed up throughout the night. Phil later compared my snoring favourably to the Symphony of Fire.

Just before daylight, thanks to my aging prostate, I rolled out of bed early, fired up the wood stove and got dressed. The ventilation of the cabin was first class: the water pail had two inches of ice on it, so we were surely in no danger of dying from lack of fresh air. With the smell of fresh coffee drifting around the shack, Phil's sleeping bag soon began to move and in a short while his nose and eyes appeared from a small opening.

"It's still dark out!" he croaked.

"You'd better get your sorry ass out of bed. Your pancakes are almost ready!"

We soon had breakfast out of the way and, as I washed the dishes, Phil wrote in his journal. He wanted to submit the story to Hunt Magazine.

With daylight coming on, I set up my spotting scope and tripod in the cabin doorway so that I could enjoy my coffee by the fire. I quickly scanned the mountain across the lake through my bino's and picked up a herd of caribou half way up the mountain. I focussed the scope on the herd and counted fifteen or twenty cows and calves and three or four bulls. As I studied them, the two larger bulls suddenly went to war, pushing and lunging, all the while spinning around and ripping clods of moss up through the snow.

I said, "Well, Phil, there's your bull."

He looked up from his journal and said, "Bull shit!"

"I'm serious. There's a herd of caribou up there on the mountain and two bulls are fighting right now!"

He came over to the door and sat down in front of the scope.

"Holy Shit," he cried, "there's a whole herd of them up there! Those bulls are monsters, Fergie!"

"I won't know if they're even legal until I have a good look at them. They need to show five good points on top before you can take one. When they stop fighting, let me back in behind the scope."

When the bulls separated I zoomed the scope up from twenty to thirty power and had a closer look. I said, "That skinny old bull with the white mane is legal and he's still the herd bull. The one he's been fighting with is younger and has a fantastic rack. It's high, wide and heavy, but I can only make out four points on top."

By this time Phil was wired and ready for action. "If that old bull is legal, he looks fine to me. I think he's beautiful!"

"OK," I said, "We'll idle up there and have a better look. In the meantime, we may run into something you like even more."

We loaded our packs with a few meat bags, sandwiches, water, cameras and optics. At the lake with a dirty, raw wind howling at our backs, we rolled the little twelve foot skiff over and slid it out onto the ice. I placed the oars into the oarlocks and said, "Jump in, Phil!" He climbed in and sat on the back seat. I set my pack in, pushed her out a little farther and stepped in. With our combined weight concentrated in one place, the band of inch thick ice along the shore began to crack and break away. We were soon moving at a good clip across the quarter mile of choppy water. On the eastern shore, with the skiff pulled out onto the grass, we got into our packs and headed up the mountain.

At the edge of the scattered timber, which started about fifty yards above the lake, I cut a five foot long stick that I could use to knock the snow from the lower branches so that we wouldn't get wet too early in the day. Within half an hour, we had reached timberline and the sun was peeping through the ragged clouds from time to time, bringing us a bit of warmth in spite of the brisk wind. We worked our way up the south side of a narrow creek where the wind had blown the ground clean of snow during the night. As we rounded the toe of a low, grassy ridge to our right, we came upon the source of the creek. It looked as if another piece of the mountainside had moved a few hundred feet down slope and then stopped allowing a marsh to form in the cavity behind it.

Directly in front of us, where the marsh drained toward the creek on our left, the fresh snow was criss-crossed with fresh moose tracks. I turned to Phil and whispered, "There's some moose right here in front of us some place ... probably over there in those thick balsams. The wind's blowing straight at them, so get ready in case a big bull moves out."

We didn't have long to wait. I caught a movement in the low balsam as a cow drifted quietly along the far side to our right. I nudged Phil "If there's a bull here, he'll be right behind her."

Suddenly Phil grabbed my arm. "Fergie, a bull!"

"He's too little, Phil. He's only got four or five points on each side. He'll be big enough in two more years."

"My God, man," Phil cried. "He's huge! I can't imagine what he'll be like when he gets big!"

The fat cow trotted purposefully up over the ridge to our right with the young bull following, all the while calling in a high pitched, whining voice. Phil stood there, mouth agape, his oil temperature in the red. I put my hand on his shoulder and said, "C'mon, Phil, we've got an appointment with a nice caribou up here."

About three hundred yards farther up the mountain stood a prominent rocky knob where we hoped to work out our final strategy. As we continued climbing, by then well above the timberline, the wind became noticeably stronger and drifting snow began to obscure our vision. Phil, a heavy smoker, was showing signs of exhaustion despite our easy pace. At one point, only fifteen yards below the lookout point, he stopped and said, "Fergie, I can't make it. I think I'm getting hypothermia."

I stood about thirty feet above him in knee-deep, drifted snow and said, "Take it easy, Phil. You'll be OK We'll take as long as we have to."

"No, I'm serious. I can't make it," he gasped.

I stood facing downhill into the stinging snow and said, "Can you take just one step?"

He looked up and said, "Yes."

"Show me." He looked at me as if I were crazy, and I said, "Go ahead — take a step!" He took one step up, then looked up at me. "How did that feel?" I asked.

"It was okay," he answered.

"Well, that's good!" I said. "Now take another one, and when you feel damn good and ready, take another one after that. Anyone can climb a mountain if they want to, but you still have to go one step at a time!" I waited until he was standing right beside me and said, "Okay, Phil, you're

152

doing great. When we hit the top of this little pitch you may have a shot at your bull."

I was beginning to get a bit of a chill myself but didn't dare let him know lest he should panic and run off down the mountain. I approached the hump carefully and, in a single step, had the entire herd in sight at just under three hundred yards. The cows and calves were feeding on the side of a ridge across a wide, flat-bottomed basin. The bulls, four of them, were actively patrolling the outside of the herd, each hoping to be the centre of attraction when the girls felt it was "party time".

Although the annual rut was barely underway, the rigors of gathering and protecting his harem had already taken their toll on the old herd bull. He was gaunt as a greyhound, and had quit feeding altogether, standing motionless with a hump in his back and his head hanging down.

The other three bulls, on the other hand, fed along contentedly around the outside of the herd, all the while staying healthy and keeping their strength up. The old bull was watching like a hawk and, when the young wide beamed bull got too close to one of his cows, suddenly charged at him with a burst of speed that certainly caught me by surprise, given his sorry condition.

This little flurry of action gave the other bulls a chance to dart in and try for a few cows but, with an incredible display of stamina, the old bull charged straight back up the side of the steep ridge and ran them off.

At this point there was no doubt in my mind that most herd bulls never make it much beyond the end of the rut as he stood there with his head down and mouth wide open, flanks heaving in and out as he struggled for breath.

With Phil prone at my side I set up the spotting scope and had a good look at the heavy beamed young bull. "No, he's not legal, Phil. The only shootable bull is the old guy. He's well past his prime and not very big in the antler department, but he will still make a nice mount. It's up to you, we've still got a few days to find you something bigger."

"Hell no!" he said. "I think he's perfect! I'd be more than happy to take him home."

"Okay," I said, "dig the snow out of your scope and get ready to shoot." The wind on top of the rocky hump was blowing furiously and the drifting snow was stinging the left sides of our faces as I shoved my old Trapper Nelson pack frame in front of Phil for a rest. He was using a .30-06 loaded with 180 grain bullets, which I thought were too heavy, but that's what we had to work with.

153

Fig 33:
Phil Morton high on the mountain with his bull caribou.

When he had settled into position, I said, "Okay, Phil, he's perfectly broadside so hold about two inches over the top of his back." He started the squeeze and there was a 'pop'. The sound of the shot was muffled by the snow and howling wind, and through the scope I saw the snow kick up under the bull's brisket.

"You're hitting low, Phil," I said. "Aim about a foot over his back." I don't know where he aimed but the next bullet hit in the same place.

With the second shot the herd began to move over the ridge into a steep but grassy draw out of the wind. I said, "Hold it, we'll let them move into that draw, then we'll pull another sneak on them. I don't think they even know you shot at them. They hear thunder in these mountains all the time."

In the ten minutes that we waited for them to drop out of sight, we damn near froze to death. I said, "Let's go, Phil. If we hurry you should get a good close shot, and the climb should warm us up."

We crossed the flat ground quickly and were part-way up the side of the ridge when I spotted the tips of caribou antlers. Instead of making good time along the top of the ridge, where the snow had blown off, we were forced to drop over the side where the snow had drifted nearly

Fig 34:
Pat Ferguson heading down the mountain.

waist deep. Phil was beginning to power out again so I said to him, "Just take your time and step right in my tracks. Keep moving, though, so you don't get cold."

I made a quick burst for about a hundred yards up the ridge and then crawled up over the top to see if we were gaining on the herd. They were less than fifty yards below me, feeding uphill on my side of the draw. And my hunter was a hundred yards behind me, played out.

I crawled back out of sight and coaxed Phil the last thirty yards to where I sat. I had to get another fifty yards out of him before he'd have a good shot. I put my hand on his shoulder and said, "Phil your bull is less than a hundred yards from us, but his cows are feeding slightly uphill and across the draw. If we make one more short burst we'll be in position for a good shot. What do you think?"

He half stood and half sat there in snow over his waist, looking much like a human version of the old bull over the ridge. I wasn't too sure if he just wanted to lie down and die quietly in the snow. His face looked waxy and pale and I thought, Christ, if he dies up here, I won't have anyone to play crib with tonight. Then I thought, he ain't gonna' die ... he likes my cooking too much!

Finally, he got a little colour back in his face and said, "OK, Fergie, let's give it one last shot."

I said, "Give me your pack so I'll have it in position to shoot when you get there." I took his rifle while he struggled out of his pack, then handed

155

it back to him. With his pack in my right hand, I struggled another fifty yards up the side of the ridge, then crossed over the top on my belly.

By this time most of the cows were feeding out of the wind on the far side of the draw, less than two hundred yards away. The big, beamy bull was feeding just to the left of them on the next ridge, while the old bull simply stood motionless at the lower end of the herd with his head hanging down.

As Phil crawled up behind me in the snow, the younger bull suddenly spotted us and froze like a statue, staring a hole in us. With his rifle in position, I said "Okay, Phil ... he's not much over one hundred and fifty yards, so aim for the centre of his lungs." He quickly started the squeeze and, at the shot, the old bull took a single step forward and just stood there. "Good shot, Phil," I said, "you got both lungs! Watch him now; he'll tip over to our side like an old sawhorse!"

In a few seconds his antlers began to tip, then over he went. The younger bull, who had watched the whole performance, then charged down off the ridge, rounded up his new harem and herded them up the mountain. I was happy in knowing that with his genetics he would make a much better herd bull.

We stood up and I shook Phil's hand. "Good work, partner, did you get your money's worth?"

He grinned a very tired grin and said, "Never in my wildest dreams could I imagine myself doing what we just did!"

We walked across the draw toward the old bull and suddenly, where a few minutes before the place had been a mass of moving caribou, everything became very quiet. I let him spend a few minutes alone with his bull while I readied my camera and tripod, then I stepped up for a look. We checked him from head to hoof, then rolled him over and checked his other side. We were shocked that an animal in his condition was still alive, let alone chasing other bulls away from his cows. He had several deep punctures through his ribs and flanks, which indicated that he had likely been fighting two or three bulls at a time. He was obviously in the process of dying a terrible death when we found him.

We made it back to camp just before dark that night and, just for the hell of it, I cooked a few caribou chops "A La Rut" for Phil — this time he really and truly had a reason to gag and retch.

•••

14
High Tension Grizzlies...

It was mid-September when my good friend Dave Brown and his wife, Elsie, showed up in Stewart for a visit. I was out of work and nearly flat broke, so I suggested that we head north and see if we could find a moose to take up some of the space in my freezer. My older son Mike had been on a sheep hunt in August but Chuck, my youngest, hadn't been in the mountains since the year before. I was about to fix that. When he headed off to school that day I said, "Talk to your teachers today. Chuck, and see if they'll give you enough homework to last you all next week." He did and they did. They had finally come to the conclusion that the Ferguson kids would be missing a little school during hunting season whether they approved or not.

We gathered up a little gear and threw a grub box together. By the end of the day we had everything loaded in the back of the old Toyota. As usual, the drive to Dease Lake was rough and dusty but the incredible fall colours made it all bearable. Shortly after noon we arrived at the home of our good friends Myles and Sherry Bradford, well established outfitters in the area. Sherry called Myles on the radio to let him know we were in Dease. He wasn't going to fly home that night until he found out we had brought strawberries from Ida's garden and a bucket of ice cream.

That night just at dark Myles came rumbling in over the ridge in his de Havilland Beaver and set it on the water as if he knew what he was doing. We all walked down to the beach to greet him as he drifted quietly into shore. I always expect Myles to look rough in the fall because he works so damn hard. This time it seemed as if he had really put himself through it. His thick dark hair was long and shaggy, he hadn't shaved in a week and was so skinny I could hear his bones rattling together. He had obviously been giving his hunters all they had paid for and more. He put his plane to bed and we all headed up to the house for a beer.

He said, "What are you guys up to, Ferg? Are you looking for a moose?"

"We sure are," I answered, "My deep freeze is nearly empty."

He said, "I can take you out and drop you off at one of my camps if you like. I've got one that I won't be using for a week or two." I accepted his generous offer and we visited on into the night. In the morning, after breakfast, we threw our meagre gear into the Beaver and were on our way. It's always nice flying with Myles because he is so at ease behind the controls.

The plane ride was short but entirely enjoyable and we were soon throwing our gear onto the shore. Before pushing off Myles said, "Good luck guys. There's a radio in the cookshack if you need to get in touch with me." We watched him take off then carried our gear up to the cabin.

Dave stepped through the kitchen door then turned to me with a big grin, "Damn! It just don't get any better than this." He had been on a few tough trips with me in the past but was really looking forward to this one. We got the eighteen foot cedar canoe down from its hanger on the side of the cabin and carried it down to the water. Chuck and Dave grabbed their fishing poles and headed out to catch our dinner. Meanwhile, I unpacked our grub box and cleaned up the kitchen. (There had been a mouse in the house.)

It wasn't long before Chuck and Dave came back with six fat grayling and a husky appetite. I had the potatoes peeled and peas in the pot so, after a quick filleting job, lunch was on its way. I rolled the fillets in flour, corn meal, lemon pepper and seasoning salt then fried them gently in real butter. Talk about living it up. Two hours after arriving at the lake we're enjoying a meal fit for royalty.

Late in the afternoon we paddled down the lake to the base of a little hill. Here we pulled the canoe quietly up into the stunted willows and climbed up the grassy hillside to sit and glass. Although the sun was breaking through the thin cloud layer the air was chilly. The surrounding mountains were covered in a fresh blanket of snow right down to the timberline which, in this case, was nearly at the valley bottom.

We spotted game almost immediately. On the sunny slope of a snowy basin five miles to the east lay a herd of about twenty caribou. With the spotting scope cranked up to thirty power, I could make out the herd bull bedded with his cows. Even at this distance it was easy to tell that he was of trophy quality. As I struggled to study him through the shimmering heat waves something caught my attention on the skyline behind him. It was another big bull and he was headed straight for the bedded herd below. We began to anticipate a bull fight but to our amazement he strode boldly down through the bedded cows and parked himself only a stones throw from the other bull. These two handsome gentlemen had likely spent the whole summer together fighting flies on a high mountain snow patch. In a few days they would be trying to kill each other over the lovely ladies now gathered around them.

On another mountainside to the south we spotted more caribou. This group of a dozen or so animals was only three miles away and was made up mostly of young bulls. A few hundred yards below the herd a good sized grizzly was digging for marmots. A loud splashing noise suddenly caught our attention five hundred yards across the lake. It was a big bull moose and judging by the way he marched into the lake, he considered himself the undisputed stud duck in these parts. As he continued on across the lake a few hundred yards away Chuck said, "Dad, aren't you going to shoot him?"

I answered, "No, Chuck, I don't think we want him real bad. He's been rutting hard for awhile now. Look at his flanks, he looks like a grey-hound. Besides he's too close to trophy size and Myles might skin us all if we take him." His antler palms were wide and somewhat rippled. Instead of laying out flat they curved up into more of a basket rack like those of a southern moose. I judged him to be around the fifty inch wide mark, the minimum width Myles will let a client take. (Myles once showed me a beautiful fifty three inch Moose that one of his hunters had taken that went fairly high in the record book.)

Just before dark a young bull followed a lone cow out into the shallow water at the south end of the lake. He had about three or four points on each side and appeared to be exactly what we were looking for except that he was a fifteen minute canoe paddle away. We watched them feed for a few minutes then paddled quietly back to camp under the cover of darkness.

At first light Dave and I enjoyed a cup of coffee and Chuck, a cup of hot chocolate, as we glassed the shores for moose. The night had been typically chilly and the mist was rising from the water as the first rays of sun touched the snow covered mountain tops. A big cow moose at the north end of the lake fed quietly in the low willows as her two calves explored the sandy beach Another cow and calf drifted into sight from behind a low ridge at the north west corner of the lake. She carried on down the gentle slope toward the end of the lake until she spotted the other cow two hundred yards away. She stopped, sized up the situation and began to feed in the willows. Her calf, in the meantime, had spotted the other two calves and ran down the hill to greet them with a high pitched Blah, Blah, Blah. The twins obviously didn't want to play as they immediately lined up shoulder to shoulder and charged at the lonesome calf with their ears laid back and front feet striking out. It quickly spun around and scrambled back to it's mother, wailing loudly in protest all the way. As the frightened calf ran past his mother, she laid back her ears and with a most sinister scowl, sent the two playground bullies back to their mother.

159

It looked as though the fog would hang over the area for awhile so we decided to take a little tour up the mountain for caribou. We threw a little grub into our packs and headed for the timberline to the east. A few hundred yards out of camp we hit fresh grizzly tracks in the patchy snow. Three miles and a gallon of sweat later we topped out onto the tundra and were soon sitting back in the warm sun enjoying the view. The caribou herd that we had spotted the night before had moved on, and so, after cooling down from the long climb, we headed around the north end of the mountain. The snow was about five inches deep, three days old and absolutely covered in caribou tracks.

We circled the entire north end of the mountain without finding a single animal. About 2:00 PM we crossed our own tracks and set out for a prominent ridge to the south. From this ridge we were able to see for five miles along the western slope. We glassed, but in vain. The herd had moved and we were too far from camp to go looking for them. Instead we spent the rest of the afternoon glassing the valley below for moose.

We returned to the camp late in the afternoon. Chuck and Dave paddled out and caught us another string of fat grayling, while I peeled the potatoes. We enjoyed another superb meal in paradise. After dinner I lit the propane light for Chuck so he could do some of his homework. While Dave washed the dishes, I got the crib board ready. We had a pot of tea, played a few games of crib, and then gave up for the night.

Morning was clear and cold again , so we paddled quietly to the south end of the lake in hopes of finding the young bull moose. A few cows and calves showed up, but not a single bull. We moved back up the lake to our own lookout hill where we stayed for the rest of the day. Chuck and Dave caught a few more grayling and some lake trout for our supper while I kept glassing. I finally spotted a big cow far up the valley and heading north. Right behind her was my fat young meat bull. We headed back to camp early and cooked up a big dinner.

We all stood out on the point listening for "moose talk" as darkness closed in. We soon heard it: a bull was grunting in the scattered timber behind camp. I pulled on my boots, pushed the canoe into the water and paddled across the lake to the place where the cows and calves had been feeding. I stepped out in the shallow water and pulled the canoe sideways to the beach, letting it rest quietly on the sand. Then I walked down the beach a short distance and listened for the bull. Hearing nothing, I cupped my hands around my mouth, squeezed my nose shut and let out a short cow call. I waited about fifteen seconds and let out another one, this time louder and longer. I moved up the beach, still in the water and gave out my very best "get your butt over here, I'm in love" cow call. Finally, I scooped up a double handful of water and let it pour back into the lake. That had to be all a self-respecting bull could take … I paddled quietly back across the lake and went to bed.

We were up and ready for action before daylight. I stood by the window sipping coffee and staring into the predawn darkness with my bino's. I could barely make out a few details along the beach four hundred yards away. One particular light coloured patch caught my eye but I couldn't figure it out. I wondered if it could be a willow branch sticking up with leaves still hanging from it. After staring at it for about ten minutes I realized it was a moose antler.

"Moose," I said, "right at the end of the lake." Within a few minutes we were able to make out the whole animal through the bino's. I told Dave, "You and Chuck can help me get the canoe in the water and then come back up and watch from the cabin. When I shoot, you can bring the packs and a bit of grub; we'll be there all day."

We got the canoe into the water without making any noise and I was soon on my way across the lake. The bull had moved up the creek a few hundred yards since we first sighted him, so I was hidden from view by the low willows along the beach. At the far shore I repeated the routine of beaching the canoe from the night before. This time, standing on the beach I could see the tops of his antlers, as he stood motionless by the creek.

A low tundra-covered ridge ran parallel to the west side of the willow bottom. I intended to work my way through a low saddle and up onto the back side of the ridge. Everything went perfectly and, as I eased over the crest of the ridge, I discovered the object of the bull's attention. An absolutely gorgeous cow moose and calf were standing in the creek nibbling on the soft willow tips along the edge, while the bull stood on top of the bank giving her googley eyes from less than a moose nose away. As she reached out for a tender branch directly at his feet he slowly lowered his nose toward hers. She bashfully pulled back for a few seconds, and then, stretching out her neck, sniffed his nose, turned, and walked out of the creek toward me. The old gentleman didn't move an inch, but watched as she stopped again to feed. At that point I recognized him as the bull that crossed the lake in front of us on the first day.

By this time the cow and calf were about one hundred and fifty yards out to my left front and the bull was about two hundred straight away. I was sure that the bull would move closer, so I got down and crawled to where I could manage a clear shot. At a low bump on the ridge I stopped and pushed my custom-built .338 into position. Just then the bull stepped down into the creek and crossed to my side, walking slowly toward the cow. When he stopped, I had the crosshairs settled on the top half of his lungs. At the shot he wheeled on his hind legs, ran back toward the creek, and stopped. I didn't want him to step ahead and fall into the water, so I held just above his neck and squeezed off another round. At the impact he dropped like a sack of moose meat.

I stood up and watched the cow and calf trot up the valley, then looked back down toward the lake. Dave and Chuck were standing on the beach waiting for my signal. I hollered at them to bring the canoe up the creek, and headed down the hill to my bull.

It was easy to see that he had been in a few battles. His antlers tips were broken in places and a hole was pushed completely through one palm. His body fat was all gone, but thankfully he didn't stink.

It was only four hundred yards to the lake as the raven flies, but Dave and Chuck had to paddle over a mile of meandering creek to get to the bull. When they arrived we set up the camera and took a few photos. I wanted to save the cape for my taxidermist; I worked on that while the boys skinned the back half. Within a few hours we had all of the meat laid out crusting up in the cool, dry air.

After resting our tired backs for some time, we loaded the meat into the canoe on a thick bed of green willow sticks. As the load got heavier, we pushed the canoe farther out into the water. With the antlers, meat, cape, our gear and ourselves on board we had about two inches of freeboard left. We made it back to camp without an impromptu bath and had the meat stacked to cool by midday. Chuck paddled back out and caught a few more grayling and we celebrated over a late lunch.. Once again I would have meat in my freezer and after the work of the great equalizer, (the meat grinder) it would even be tender.

I spent the rest of the day BS'ing with Dave and working on the cape; splitting the lips, turning the ears, and finally, salting it down. Chuck, meanwhile, kept himself occupied with his grayling-culling program out on the lake.

Late in the afternoon Myles flew in for a visit in his Super Cub. He walked up to the antlers, took a quick look, and said, "Dammit, Ferg, when I flew over and saw these big palms, I thought that I was going to have to give you shit!" We all had a good laugh, knowing that Myles wouldn't let one of his hunters shoot a bull that small.

Myles wanted to know what my plans were now that I had my meat. "Well," I answered, "I'm in no big panic, so we can fly out whenever it fits in with your schedule."

Fig 35:
Dave Brown and Chuck Ferguson preparing to head down the creek.

"OK. I'm in a bit of a tight spot right now. I had two hunters cancel their trip a while back and I booked two more in their place. Now the first two guys are back on board again, so I'm a little short of guides. Do you think you can stick around for a while?"

"Sure," I replied. "I can stay. Dave and Chuck can get the meat home all right."

"Good," he said. "I'll bring your hunter and your guide's license by sometime tomorrow, and fly Dave and Chuck to Dease Lake. This guy is looking for a grizzly and this country is crawling with them, so your chances are fairly good."

That night we all had a good visit, Dave and I playing crib, and Chuck doing homework. We drifted off to sleep to the mournful howling of a pack of wolves across the lake.

During the night, the weather changed. The high pressure system had moved on, taking its clear, sunny skies. It was replaced by storm clouds bringing snow flurries and gusting winds. Dave and I got to work packing up his gear for the flight out while Chuck headed for the canoe. He wanted to catch a few more fish for Dave to take home. He had just begun to paddle out to his favourite spot when a nasty snow storm swooped down on him. Chuck, not one to be bothered by a few billion snow flakes, carried on to his fishing hole unconcerned. At times, we could barely make him out as he fought the wind, waves and, of course, the driving snow.

He stuck with it for about a half hour, and then, about the time the storm blew over, headed for shore. I whipped him up a mug of hot chocolate, and when he came through the door of the cabin, traded it to him for seven fat grayling.

Myles flew in at mid-day, dropped off my hunter, and hauled Dave and Chuck to Dease Lake. Don and I got acquainted as we organized his gear in the cabin, In BC, it is unlawful to hunt within six hours of being airborne in an aircraft other than a regularly scheduled aircraft.

As luck would have it, Don was also a fisherman, so we slipped the canoe into the water and paddled out to catch our supper. It wasn't long before we were headed back to shore with four nice grayling. I cooked up another big meal. Don thought he has died and gone to heaven. Evening was closing in on us so I said, "Come on, Don, let's go up on the hill behind the cabin and have a little look around." We took out bino's and spotting scopes, settling in about fifty yards up the slope. It was nearly dark before we spotted anything, and when we did our excitement level went through the roof. A big boar mountain grizzly was on my moose kill. He must have just gotten there, because I had glassed the area several times. I set up the old Bushnell spotting scope and got focused on him just in time for him to raise his big black head. He was looking directly toward the cabin from half a mile away as he munched away on the scraps. We watched him feed until dark then left him to his prize and went to bed.

In the morning the BC-Yukon Air Services Otter flew in with three resident hunters and off loaded them half way down the lake. I didn't want them to come up to our end of the lake and scare the bear away. When they launched their canoe, Don and I launched ours and made an appearance out on the water. They immediately saw us and headed for the south end of the lake. Don and I had supper early after a day-long vigil in the event that we found ourselves occupied just before dark. The weather was improving with the wind blowing out of the north again, so, as the sun dipped in the west, we got ready for action.

About the time I thought he wouldn't show, there he was, smacking his lips, munching on moose scraps, and all the while staring straight toward the cabin. Don and I quietly slipped the canoe into the water and crossed the lake. Once on the far shore, we made our way carefully around the back side of the ridge where I had shot the moose. We moved very cautiously over the top until we spotted him. He was quite a sight, ripping away at the carcass and glaring around suspiciously.

I looked at Don and his eyeballs were nearly touching his glasses. I put my hand on his shoulder and whispered, "How are you doing, Don?"

"OK, I think." He answered not taking his eyes from the boar. I noticed that the bear had dragged the carcass away from the creek a short distance. I suspected he was trying to distance himself either from the lingering human scent or the cabin. In any event, the shot would not be as far as I had anticipated. We got down and crawled along the soft moss and grass until we were well beyond the crest of the ridge and pretty much in full view of the boar. Don carefully moved his rifle into position and tucked his jacket in under it for a rest. I snuggled in behind my .338 to see what my sight picture would look like. It looked good. "OK, Don." I whispered, "How does it look? Do you have a clear shot at his lungs?" He looked straight ahead nodding his head in nervous silence. "OK," I whispered, "Take your time and squeeze the shot. As soon as you shoot, I'm going to give him the works, so don't stop shooting until he's down." Again he nodded his head.

I placed my cross hairs back on the boar, eased off the safety and waited. At the shot the boar went into a violent spin then turned to run up the creek, venting a hair-raising roar. I picked him up again in my cross hairs and squeezed off a round. The impact of the 210-grain Nosler partition knocked him off his feet. He was back up and scrambling to our left only partly visible in the low willows. He ran into the middle of a big ox-bow, jumped straight into the deep water and swam across. As the far bank he struggled to pull himself up but couldn't make it. It was then I realized that his hind end wasn't working too well. "Come on, Don," I said. "Let's go finish him quick!"

We hurried down the hill and across the soggy willow bottom toward the boar. When I came out on to the grassy edge of the creek I was about a hundred feet from him. He was quiet by then but still trying to pull himself up the undercut bank with his front feet. I waited for Don to catch up to me then whispered, "We'll get up close and I'll get him to chase me. When he comes out this side of the creek you can whack him, OK?" By this time Don was nearly hyperventilating. I took him by the arm and pulled him with me as I moved toward the boar. At thirty feet I stopped and whispered, "Stay right here and let's see what happens." I moved ahead another thirty feet until I was straight across from him. A quick look down into the water told me that it was very deep on my side as well. The boar, meantime, was strangely quiet except for his heavy breathing. He had to know I was standing quietly twenty feet behind him, but he kept looking straight ahead. I looked at Don and nodded my head. He nodded back.

In a low voice I said, "Hey big guy, I'm right here behind you." He turned his head and body slowly to the left until he looked right at me. As he began to swim across toward me, he locked his eyes onto mine with the most hateful glare I could ever have imagined. He was looking right into my soul. When he was less than ten feet from my boots I glanced toward Don and much to my dismay he was headed toward Watson Lake. I ran after him yelling, "Don, Stop!" I caught up to him easily as by this time his hind legs weren't working too well either. I got a firm grip on his arm and glanced back at the boar who was now ripping out clods of grass and willow clumps in his frustrated efforts to pull himself up the bank. "Come on, Don." I said "he can't make it out. You'll have to shoot him in the water." I practically had to skid him up to the boar who was roaring furiously again. I pointed to the lung area (it was the biggest target) and said, "Right there on his lungs, Don, about an inch above the water." Don quickly fired and the brave boar let out one final valiant roar as he slid beneath the surface of the water with the last rays of sunset reflecting from his hate-filled eyes.

A deafening silence closed in on us as we stood staring down into the dark water. My knees began to feel a little shaky and I was sure Don was feeling a little drained himself. We found a soft grassy hump to sit on near the edge of the creek. "What happened to your first shot, Don?" I asked "He sure as hell wasn't hit in the lungs or he wouldn't have gone fifty feet."

"I'm not sure." He said, "But I think I clipped a bush about twenty feet in front of my gun barrel."

We sat quietly as the evening sounds slowly came back with the song of a loon far down the lake. I thought about the many black bears and grizzlies I had hunted and guided for over the years. Most of them were clean, one-shot kills where the bears nearly always made a short panic run before piling up. Only one other time did I have a screw-up that involved a hunter with a .340 Weatherby Magnum who was more frightened of it's violent recoil than he was of the better than seven-foot black bear I had put him on. Fortunately I had my trusty .234 to back him up.

It was nearly black dark by the time we got back to the canoe. The moon was just coming up; it would only be a short time before we could see well again. We pointed the canoe up the creek and paddled for nearly an hour up its wandering course before we finally reached the spot where I thought the bear rested on the bottom. With the canoe paddle I probed into the water as we moved slowly along until I hit a big lump. I quickly rolled up my sleeve and plunged my left arm into the water to my shoulder. It was the bear so, with a fist full of hair and a mighty heave, I moved him far enough off the bottom to get a grip on him with both hands. Don tried to keep the canoe balanced while I struggled with the chore of getting his big head up. With a length of rope I fastened a loop around his thick neck and threw a couple of half hitches around his snout. I took a couple of wraps around the centre spreader of the canoe and gave the end of the rope to Don. I took the boar by both sides of the head and heaved back for all I was worth as Don pulled in the slack. It worked. We had him up off the creek bottom and were drifting down stream with the current.

We went ashore at the same sandbar where I had loaded our moose meat. We pulled the boar up as far as we could into the shallow water, and then, standing in the deep water behind him, we rolled him one turn into about four inches of water. It was then that I got the clever idea to take the whole boar back to camp un-skinned. We moved the canoe into position on its side with both the bears' left legs inside. Then, with a loud grunt, we rolled the whole shebang back into the deep water. I heard a loud snap as the weight of the bear cracked the spreader bar, but it all held together. We were soon drifting quietly down the creek in the moonlight with less than two inches of freeboard. Thankfully, there was no wind, or we would surely have been swamped when we entered the lake.

At our docking site, the bright moonlight sparkled on the frosted grass. I got Don to hold the bow rope from shore then, standing at the edge of the water, I, gently pushed the heavy load back out into the water. When the rope came tight I said, "Go," and Don took off on the run. As the canoe came by me I grabbed it and pulled for all I was worth. Much to our surprise it shot out onto the slippery grass almost by itself, running over me in the process. We tipped the bear out of the canoe and with one last heave, rolled him onto his belly, so he would look nice for photos in the morning. We both washed our hands in the lake and then I turned to Don and said, "Congratulations, Don. That was one hell of an adventure!" It was 1:00 am.

Morning dawned clear and cold as we washed down our breakfast with my favourite version of cowboy coffee. (It's a lot like other coffee except for the addition of a few spruce needles and mouse turds.) We had just gotten the camera and tripod set up by the bear when we picked up the familiar sound of the Beaver as it rounded a peak to the north. As Myles circled to land, Don and I took a whole mess of photos of ourselves with the frost-covered bear. He was nearly black with just a hint of cinnamon tip on his hump — typical for a large boar grizzly in these parts.

Fig 36:
"He was nearly black with just a hint of cinnamon tip on his hump..."

As the plane drifted toward us, Myles stepped out of the cabin, fastened a rope onto the toe of the float and jumped ashore. "It looks like you guys may have had some kind of an adventure." he said as Sherry and son, Leland, who was about twelve years old at the time, climbed out of the plane.

"Yes we did." answered Don "We had as much adventure as most sane people can handle." We related the whole story to them as Myles examined the bear from end to end. Sherry took one look at his face and shuddered.

"I think this is the same bear that kept me treed on the cabin roof for most of the day a couple of years back." She said. "He kept standing up and putting his front feet on the roof. It still gives me chills when I remember the evil look on his face when he looked into my eyes." Sherry is one of the most strong-willed women I had ever met. To hear her express any kind of fear at all caught me by surprise.

She walked up to the cabin to make us another coffee while Myles and Leland helped us with the very awkward job of skinning the stiffened bear.

As we finished up our little chore Myles said, "I've got another grizzly hunter waiting for you over at the other camp. He twisted a knee cartilage on his caribou hunt, so he's been resting for a few days." Then he said something that really caught my attention. "Remember that big grizzly that I told you about. The one that keeps tearing our other camp apart?"

"The one Butch and I cleaned up after when he threw the kitchen stove out through the window?" I asked.

"That's the one," he said. "I think he's the one that's got a big bull moose buried in the middle of that long meadow below camp. The boys spotted the kill when they rode by on the horse trail yesterday. All they could see was a big pile of grass pulled up with a big antler palm sticking out of it."

Was I ready to go? Hell yes! If, in fact, this was the same bear he was big, old and smart, because he had been causing everyone grief for several years and we hadn't been able to corner him.

After coffee, we cleaned up camp, packed our gear and the bear hide and a flew back to the other camp. I spent the rest of the day splitting the lips, turning the ears and finishing the feet.

My next grizzly hunter, Gene, and his partner, John sat and visited with me as I worked on the hide in front of the cook shack. Sitting beside me, working on a mountain goat cape, was Lester Frank, a fine, young, native guide, who had been working for Myles for a few years. He was a good man with pack horses and the hunters all liked him

Late in the afternoon, after Lester and I had salted down our hides, we threw a little gear together in preparation for our three-mile stroll down the horse trail to the meadow. We didn't want to take the horses as they would make too much noise and alert the bear to our presence. We were all nervous as we headed out of camp, Lester and the young wrangler Russell in the lead followed by Gene, John and myself. For twenty minutes, we walked in silence until we broke out of the poplars onto an open south-facing slope.

We all sat down and pulled out our bino's. Lester said, "Fergie, you see those tall cottonwoods down there by the horse trail?" I nodded and he said, "Look at the top of that tallest tree. That dark spot on the meadow behind it is the kill." I set up the spotting scope and, sure enough, there was an exceptionally large antler palm sticking up out of the mound.

I said, "What do you think, Lester? Do you suppose that bull was wounded by another one before the grizzly killed him?"

"Oh, probably." He said. "It happens all the time. Sometimes when they fight a bull get hooked in the guts and a grizzly can smell that for a long way off." I said, "Do you remember that helicopter pilot — I think his name was Carl — from Dease Lake? He flew in to a little lake on a high plateau west of Cassiar to pick up two prospectors one time and watched a really small grizzly kill a big bull moose. I guess that little bear kept charging straight into the bull and the bull would just toss it into the air like a pissed off hairy ball. The bear finally hit the bull so hard on the top of the head that he broke his neck."

Lester said, "I remember hearing about that. I heard the pilot flew by a few days later and a big dark boar was on the kill. That poor little bear probably only got one good feed before he got chased off."

We studied the area around the kill to try and figure out where the bear was lying up. A long, narrow strip of willows along the creek, and about two hundred yards south of the kill, looked like the place to me. "Where do you think he is, Lester?" I asked.

"I think he's right there in that strip of willows." He answered.

Just then a far off "awnk, awnk, awnk" reached us from across the valley over a mile away. We soon spotted a wide set of moose antlers moving toward us through the tall willows. As he moved into the open, it was easy to see, even at that distance, that the rut had not been easy on him. In contrast to his nearly sixty inch antlers, he looked like a cardboard cut-out. He appeared to be on a mission as he marched, grunting, across the valley.

If the bear was in the willows, we were sure he would be paying attention to the approaching bull moose, so we seized the opportunity to hustle down the horse trail toward the kill. Half way down the steep trail, the tall cottonwoods along the base of the hill were getting high enough to block our view of where we thought the bear was. We stopped and sat down there to watch the high drama unfold. The bull disappeared for a few minutes in the creek, but when he moved into the open on our side, he was moving along only thirty yards from the willows. Suddenly, he stopped and, with his head up at a most ridiculous angle, stared intently into the willows to his right.

Lester jerked as if he had been poked with a stock prod. "Fergie, he's there." He whispered excitedly. "I saw something black move in the willows." We kept our eyes glued to the spot until the moose moved off to our right and up the valley.

The sun was beginning to set, so we decided to get into position before the bear moved onto the kill. Lester had an elevated spot in mind where the trail crossed a ridge and we soon had the hunters in position. I whispered to Gene. "Are you OK?" He nodded his head. I looked at John and whispered "Are you ready, John?" He nodded his head. "OK, as soon as Gene fires, give him the works." John nodded his head and looked back toward the kill, which was just over a hundred yards away.

We didn't have long to wait as a big black head suddenly appeared at the edge of the willows three hundred yards away. For ten minutes the only things that moved were the bears sinister black eyes and his big black nose as he carefully tested the wind. Then, somewhat satisfied, he strode boldly across the meadow to his prize, raked back a few clods of swamp grass, and began to feed.

He was at a bad angle, so, when Gene glanced at me, I motioned for him to wait. The light was beginning to fail quickly; so as soon as he turned broadside I gave Gene the nod.

At the shot, all hell broke loose. The entire scene instantly flew into fast forward with the two magnums roaring in my ears and the big bear spinning wildly as a flurry of bullets whizzed past him. They both emptied their magazines at the same time and I hollered "Stop shooting!" as the boar, by this time, had run and jumped into the creek. I could see the top of head as he swam up the creek so I said, "John, how much ammunition do you have left?"

"I'm out." He said.

I suddenly felt sick, "Gene, how much do you have left?"

"I've got two rounds left." he answered.

"Give me your rifle, quick," I said as I grabbed his .300 and stuffed the last two rounds into the magazine. I fed the first round into the chamber, flipped on the safety and said, "Lester, you guys stay here. There's no use in all of us getting killed." I took off running down the slope toward the meadow.

I made it to the creek in time to see the boar's head disappear around the corner to the right, as he swam against the current a hundred yards ahead. The row of willows ran parallel to the creek with a twenty foot wide strip of long yellow grass in between. I ran along that strip of grass, by this time nearly winded, trying to gain some ground on the boar. At a slight curve in the creek, I stepped quietly out to the edge and there he was, less than thirty yards away, still swimming upstream. I could easily hear his heavy breathing and all indications were that his lungs were functioning just fine. I began to wonder if he had been hit at all. I stepped back out of sight and kept moving upstream as quietly as possible for another fifty yards until I came to a deep trench, where the beavers had been dragging willows into the water. On the right side of the trench stood a low hump of dirt crowned in waist-high dry grass. I stepped carefully up to the hump and immediately spotted ripples in the water, and heard his breathing directly below me. He was so close to me that I couldn't see him for the heavy grass along the bank. My lungs were still screaming for oxygen but I managed to keep my breathing to a minimum as he swam into view again at about thirty feet. I quietly raised the rifle and tried to put the cross hairs on the back of his neck but, for some reason, I was a little unsteady.

Now that I was within easy range of him, I used the chance to recharge my oxygen supply. In the meantime the boar, at a right turn in the creek, turned toward the far bank. This would likely be my last chance to get a good shot at him, so I quickly picked a shooting lane through the tall grass. At about forty yards he hit the shore and with two powerful strides was standing atop a steep mud bank glaring back in my direction. For a few long seconds he just stood there, a dripping wet mountain of muscle and pent up wild rage. I tried my best to settle the cross hairs on his lungs, only to see them waving wildly from one end of him to the other.

The next instant he was gone and I thought, "Great, here it is nearly dark and I have to cross the creek in four feet of icy water after a grizzly that I'm not sure is wounded."

Before I had a chance to make a plan, I noticed a slight movement to the left of where the boar has disappeared. Then, further to the left, I saw it again and suddenly it hit me. I was experiencing first hand the age-old grizzly tactic of setting up an ambush on his back trail. He must have been nearly crawling on his belly because I could barely make him out as he drifted silently back toward me behind the fringe of tall grass.

Directly across from me, was another two-foot-deep trench left by the beavers. When he crossed it, I would have about a five-foot-wide shooting lane. At that point he would be less than thirty feet away.

I got down on my right knee and prepared to shoot as he closed the distance. At fifty feet, I began to hear his breathing and the silent swishing of the grass. Then, like magic, he was there. I could just make out the end of his big nose and his bottom lip sticking out, as he stood there at the edge of the beaver run, looking down the creek for his pursuer. His nose was working like a big pulsating vacuum cleaner as he tried to pick up my scent. Then, silently, the big nose lowered slowly to the ground and the trap was set.

A haze of sinister calm settled over the valley as the frost and darkness closed in on me and my big cuddly friend a few feet away. I looked down into the black water and thought. "How many jumps will it take him to get to me? If he does make it into the water, I'll have to stand on the bank and try to hit him somewhere in the spinal column. If the first shot fails should I save the last one for myself?"

Fig 37:
"The big bear pounded both front feet on the grassy hump in front of him."

Almost unconsciously, I fumbled at the back of the variable scope to make double sure that it was turned down to the lowest power. Then, I slowly brought the scope up to my eye and looked at his nose. I could still see it clearly, and it looked frightening to say the least.

I took one last look around at the snow-covered mountain peaks and slowly stood up. That did it. With an ear shattering roar the big bear exploded from his hiding place and pounded both front feet down hard on the grassy hump in front of him. He took a quick glance down at the creek and as he bunched up for the jump, let out another roar. I managed to get the cross hairs on his chest and at that instant squeezed the trigger. A five-foot tongue of flame jumped out toward him and he fell back from the hump with all four feet in the air.

The roaring stopped and was replaced by the grizzly's own brand of death rattle, perhaps best described as 'teeth-popping'. It sounded like someone pounding a pair of round river rocks together. From the first time I stood up until the time he quit popping his teeth a mere four or five seconds had elapsed. The sound of the single shot echoed down the valley, and silence took hold as I stood there alone. I would liked to have crossed over the creek and sat with the old boar for a few minutes.

He died like he lived, brave and proud.

Out of the darkness, I could hear Lester and the hunters bellering, "Fergie, are you OK?" They were all fairly excited, so when I could get a word in sideways I yelled back, "I'm OK, come on down and help me skin this critter."

Gene's knee was giving him hell, so he and John stayed up on the trail while Lester and Russell made their way out onto the meadow. By the time they got to me, I had a big pile of dry willow sticks ready for a fire. Russell said, "What's that for?" I said, "That's so I can light a big fire and warm you up after you cross over and get that bear." His eyes got big and his mouth fell open. "I'm not going in that cold water." I said, "Somebody's got to and I'm holdin' the rifle, so get your clothes off." He stared at me in disbelief, glanced at Lester, and began peeling off the laundry. I said, "Leave your long johns on and maybe that big skid mark will be gone by the time you get back."

Lester and I shuddered as the kid slipped down into the chest deep ice water, all the while gasping for breath. We fed him words of encouragement, if for no other reason, to show him that he was still our buddy, after all.

At the far bank, he carefully made his way up the muddy beaver slide toward the boar, who was only ten feet away. "He's awful big. I don't know if I can even roll him." With that he got down behind the big black hulk and went to work like a little wolverine, heaving, grunting and snarling. In no time at all, he had rolled the boar to the edge of the creek.

By this time, I had the fire burning tall and hot. Russell gave the boar one last push and as he rolled into the water jumped in with him.

With his back against the current and water up to his shoulders he had a death grip on one huge front paw. Somehow, he summoned up the extra strength and courage to make his legs move and drift the completely submerged boar across to where we could help him. We finally got a rope around his neck, and, with a few more super human efforts, had him up on dry ground. Russell certainly earned his beans that time.

We got him skinned and were on our way in about 45 minutes. At the horse trail, Gene and John were cold from sitting but we took care of that right away — it was uphill all the way back to camp. Lester and Russell took off on a forced march into the moonlight, taking turns carrying the heavy pack and got to camp an hour ahead of me and the hunters.

In the morning, we laid the hide out on a fresh skiff of snow and took a few photos. Myles inspected the pelt and our 'in the dark' skinning job.

When his hand touched the area behind the hump, he said, "This is the bastard who's been tearing our camp to pieces every year. See this scar across his back? I damn near got him that time, and he's wrecked this place several times since then."

Then he turned to me and said. "Ferg, my guides spotted a big dark boar with a 60-inch moose buried in a swamp up north of here. Are you interested?"

I said, "Well Myles, I sure could use the excitement but I've got a funeral to go to." (My good friend Tommy Tompkins had just passed away.) As it turned out, Myles took the hunter out himself and got the bear.

•••

15

The Fizz Bang Moose...

The whole sequence of events started in the spring of 1993, when Rick Flynn suggested I try out his black powder gun. I wasn't overly enthusiastic about it, but for the lack of something better to do I thought, what the hell, I've got nothing to lose.

We took a spin out of Stewart to a small logging show where we could set up a target. Rick stuffed a load into his home-built cannon and passed it to me with a big grin on his face. Right away, I was on edge, not knowing what to expect. Does it kick? Is it going to blow my ear drums out? Rick was really getting a kick out of my insecurity. Normally it was me doing the chain-jerking. I passed the gun to him, put on my shooting muffs, then took it back. Under his instruction I placed a cap on the nipple, pulled the set trigger and lined up on the target. I let my breath out as I started the squeeze. When the shot came it was nothing like I had expected, but a moderately loud 'ka-blam' accompanied by a mild push and a big cloud of black powder smoke.

It was a rush. We carried on shooting for awhile, then Rick showed me how to clean the rifle properly. On the way home we talked about the different styles and calibres of rifles.

When I suggested a large calibre for moose and bear, he said, "My father-in-law out in Hazelton has a .58 Hawkin for sale. It was custom built by a guy in Smithers, but you may not want to carry it."

"Why not?" I asked.

"It weighs about 15 pounds!" Rick laughed.

I had to have a look at it, so we made the four hour trip to Hazelton and, of course, I bought it.

Before long, I had enough gear together to get the old cannon stoked up. I set up a target at ninety yards, which was as far as the local sand pit allowed, and unleashed a round ball. Right then and there I gave my new rifle its name: Rolling Thunder. I worked my powder load up until it began to burn through the patch then backed it off a bit. The whole time I was working on the sight adjustment as well. It was grouping about five inches low so after every shot I would file down the front sight a little. After about ten rounds and a couple of cleanings I had it grouping right in the bull.

I ended up working seven days a week for the rest of the spring and summer, so I was unable to do any more shooting until fall. On my return from a two and a half month drilling and blasting job near Wrangel, Alaska, I was accosted by my good friend Jim Marx. "Let's go on a moose hunt!" he said.

"Sure," I replied. "When do you want to go?"

"Tomorrow."

"OK" And that was that. I went home and threw a little gear together, explaining to Ida as I packed, the benefits of this temporary separation.

The next morning Jim, his son Dwayne and Spike, the wonder-dog, stopped to pick me up before daylight. I came out of the house with my loaded pack and the .58 in an old shotgun soft case. Jim shot me a puzzled look. "Aren't you bringing your .338 too?"

"No," I answered. "I think I'll stick to the old smoke pole and see how it works out."

"Are you sure?"

I said I was and jumped into the front passenger seat of his Ford Crew Cab. This was apparently the signal for all dogs named Spike, Brutus, Killer, etc., to rip the arm off anyone named Fergie. Jim and Dwayne got a hell of a charge out of Spike's enthusiastic welcome.

The five hour drive to Dease Lake went well. After stopping by the BC-Yukon Air Service float base to check in, we went into downtown Dease Lake for lunch. This is guaranteed always to be an adventure, since many of the local characters congregate in the coffee shop at lunch time. We weren't disappointed.

With our meal out of the way, we got back to the float base and unloaded our gear on the dock. Our timing was perfect, as Bruce McNaughton, owner/pilot of BC-Yukon Air had just finished his lunch as well.

Twenty minutes later, we were loaded up and in the air. As we gained altitude it was evident that we were in for a burst of snow. Off to the west, where we were headed, ominous black clouds were releasing white curtains across the horizon. Bruce expertly manoeuvred his trusty Otter around the scattered flurries and before long was pointing the nose down for his final approach to our chosen lake.

I looked back from my seat up front to see how Jim and Dwayne were doing. They were just fine, but I couldn't say the same for Spike. He was the greenest black dog I had ever seen in my life. He was sitting on the floor between Dwayne's legs convulsing with the dry heaves. Jim was almost in tears laughing at Dwayne, who was desperately trying to keep Spike from barfing in his lap.

Meanwhile, as Bruce concentrated on another perfect landing, I glanced out the side window and spotted a very surprised bull moose watching us from his bed. This was certainly encouraging.

Before long, all of our gear sat in a big heap on the shore and Bruce was on his way home.

As the sound of the Otter drifted away to the east, we all grabbed a load of gear and carried it up to our campsite near a patch of twisted balsam. Before we could make a second trip down to the water, we were jolted to attention by a commotion across the lake. It was the bull I had seen at the end of the lake, and he seemed determined to have a little chat with us. He grunted with every breath as he marched boldly along the far shore, three hundred yards away. Every hundred yards or so, he would suddenly stop and glare at us, then carry on down the lake to our left. It soon became apparent that he was going to cross to our side at a narrows about four hundred yards south of camp.

I said, "Jim, grab your rifle quick! We may have to shoot him in self defence." (In B.C. it's illegal to hunt wildlife within six hours of flying.)

Jim and I moved to the south of the camp as he entered the water and waited to see what would happen. Like a big ship, he drifted across the thirty-yard narrows and surged up onto the grassy point. Now standing there broadside, he looked all out of proportion. His sixty-inch antlers, with wide palms and very long points along with his huge neck and chest, didn't seem to match the part from his ribs back. His flanks were sucked up toward his backbone like a greyhound in distress. Since we were here primarily to get out winter meat, we didn't really relish the thought of having to shoot him. Of course, that didn't deter Jim from entertaining us all by hurling a spectacular display of insults in the general direction of the bull. Meanwhile, the bull, having suddenly decided that our idea of a wild time in the bush didn't match his, made himself scarce behind a low ridge, leaving us to set up our camp in peace.

We set up a big dome tent for sleeping in and, twenty feet away, we set up the kitchen tent. This was a crude structure, made up of blue and orange plastic tarps, pipe, rope, elastic bands, chewing gum, moose blood, burn holes and, if I'm not mistaken, a few bullet holes. But it worked just fine. Jim had welded together a small, functional wood stove — the kind of equipment that no man should be without in base camp. We set it up near the back wall of the kitchen tent and stuffed the stove pipe out one of the burn holes. Soon, we had the kitchen arranged to our satisfaction and headed down to the water to wrestle with another one of Jim's handy gadgets … his folding boat! We had it set up and ready to go in record time without a single life-threatening injury.

Jim also had a little chainsaw along, so we cut down a few snags, dragged then back to camp, bucked them into stove-sized chunks, and split some kindling.

By the time all the chores were done it was time for dinner. While Jim crashed around in the kitchen, Dwayne and I got right down to business with a few games of cribbage. All the while, Spike kept himself occupied by trembling, whining and growling as he stared out the door. He was absolutely positive that he was going to be wolf droppings by morning. Spike was so nervous, in fact, that he didn't even notice when his tail caught fire against the stove!

Our dinner that night was second to none. Although Jim is the closest thing to a bush ape I've ever seen, he cranked out a meal fit for real humans. Spike, on the other hand, was so nervous he couldn't keep anything down. I think he ate the same meal sixteen times. After dinner, Jim washed the dishes while Dwayne and I locked horns in a few more games of crib, by then, under lantern light. As we dealt the cards and drank hot tea, we discussed our plans for the morning. In previous years, Jim had rigged up several crude tree stands in the area, so we had various options. In the morning, we would make our choice according to the wind direction.

Sleep came easy with the sound of waves lapping against the shore and a chilly breeze whispering through the balsams. Morning found us back in the cook shack just before shooting light. Not wanting to alert the whole country with cooking smells, we all had a light snack and threw a little grub into our packs.

The three of us decided to stay together for the first morning, so I left the muzzle loader in camp. We had plenty of firepower with Dwayne's .35 Whelan and Jim's .300 Winchester magnum. The first tree stand, a big bushy jack pine, stood alone on the point of a low ridge about two hundred yards from the timber on the east and one hundred yards from the narrows on the west — the same narrows the big bull had crossed the day before.

Once in the tree, we had a perfect view of the entire lake and most of the meadows trailing back from it. Twisted willows dotted the borders of these soggy meadows, giving way to arctic birch and open patches of bunch grass farther up the slopes. The low ridges were sparsely covered with patches of balsam and a few lonely jack pines.

Jim pointed to a ridge beyond the south end of the lake. "You see that big jack pine sticking up on the west side of that ridge?" I studied it through my bino's, then looked at him. "There's a stand in that tree and in that one too," he said as he pointed to another tree across the lake. I soon spotted the rough little platform twenty feet up the tree. Then he pointed to the north end of the lake. "You see those two trees on that little hump about a mile north of the lake?" Again I took a look through my bino's. "The left tree is where I shot my moose from last year," he said with a wide grin.

"You see that thick little balsam over there by the edge of the meadow?" I said, pointing to the south-east. "That's where Dodd shot that fifty-six inch Boone and Crockett bull."

Without a doubt, we were perched like a bunch of ravens in the heart of moose heaven. We all got comfortable on our chosen branches while Jim gave a few "lovesick cow" calls. A while later he tried a few more. By mid-morning, there was no action, so Dwayne wanted to go for a little stroll. We climbed down, got back into our packs, and made our way to a small lake a mile to the south-west. We didn't want to leave our scent all over the place, but couldn't resist going over for a look anyway. We found a dry patch of grass near the timber at the north end of the lake. I gave a few calls as we had a bite to eat. Before long we were all sound asleep in the grass enjoying a rare burst of sunshine. Talk about high intensity moose hunting!

Eventually, a cloud mass moved across the sun, ruining a perfectly good snooze. It was then mid-afternoon, so we decided to hike back to camp and have dinner. That way we would be able to hunt until dark. But, as it turned out, we ended the day mooseless.

I thought it wise to load the .58 before dark so I wouldn't make any noise doing it in the morning. First, I took out my cleaning kit and swabbed any remaining oil out of the barrel. Next, I fired three caps on the nipple to burn any oil out of the flash hole. Then I dumped a pre-measured load of "Double F" down the barrel, ramming a grease-patched round on top of it.

Meanwhile, Dwayne carried in a few more loads of firewood while Jim worked his magic in the kitchen. We were soon enjoying another of his culinary delights: pork chops, beans and potatoes. It was a meal guaranteed to keep the sleeping bags fluffed up even on the coldest night.

Spike, on the other hand, still had yet to keep down any food. He was beginning to resemble a stick dog. Perhaps he was suffering from withdrawal. After all, we had neglected to bring along several of his personal effects, namely:

- his chesterfield,
- his TV, VCR and collection of *Coyote* and *Road Runner* cartoons,
- his personal trainer, Dwayne's little sister, Jody,
- and his assortment of arms and legs from the neighbour's kids.

After dinner, Dwayne and I sat by the stove and played a few games of crib while Jim took care of the dishes. Dwayne was beginning to learn a few of my dirty crib moves, and so forcing me to resort to advanced techniques in my repertoire of unscrupulous card plays. Even with these, my efforts were in vain. Dwayne kicked my sorry butt all over the board to Jim's cruel delight. As the fire burned down, we had a final cup of tea, brushed our teeth and headed for the sack.

Some time during the night, we received an inch of snow. This had us feeling fairly upbeat as we pulled on our frozen boots and crawled out of the tent. It was already light enough to get going so I asked Jim," What do you want to try today?"

"Well, he said, "I think we're going to try the big tree at the narrows. We'll take the boat in case we get a bull."

"OK! That sounds good," I said. "I'm going to try that stand at the north end. I'm feelin' kind' a moosey!"

We threw a little food and water into our packs, wished each other good luck, and headed out.

The trail I wanted to take ran along a gentle slope just fifty feet behind our camp. As I stepped out onto the trail, I saw fresh tracks in the snow, grizzly prints the size of frying pans and heading north past camp. I back-tracked him to directly above the camp to find that he had passed it by casually, telling me that he likely knew of our presence from the beginning. Having had the opportunity to observe many mountain grizzlies travelling in the fall, I was fairly certain that he was only passing by to see if we had left him a gut pile yet.

Turning north again, I had very little choice but to follow the trail if I wanted to get to my tree stand. For the first hundred yards, it wandered among scattered patches of arctic birch and bunch grass, then disappeared into a long strip of tall balsam. As I moved into the dark timber, I began to imagine hairy danger behind every tree. Two hundred yards and fifteen fun-filled minutes later, I broke out of the timber onto an open bunch grass hillside. The bear had kept to the main trail, so I broke off down another fork toward the end of the lake on my left.

Off the end of the lake, a series of terraced meadows resembling rice paddies stretched for a half mile north toward the tree stand. Each meadow was separated from its neighbour by a margin of short willows.

Feeling safer out in the open, I removed the cap from the nipple on the Hawkin and worked my way carefully across each soggy meadow. In some places the water nearly reached the top of my high rubber boots. The last meadow before the tree stand was over two hundred yards across; there was a lonely, eight-foot spruce tree standing in the middle.

I'd just slogged past the spruce when I was jolted to attention by a strange noise far off to my left. As I turned for a look, the sound hit me again. It was a bull moose grunting, but I couldn't see him yet. A few scattered willows along the western edge of the meadow were blocking my view of some parts of the mile wide valley. To the right, I could make out the south end of a small lake which I had previously seen from the air. In a few steps I spotted him. He was a half mile across the valley, walking directly toward me and grunting with every breath. His huge antlers rocked from side to side as he walked.

I was suddenly overcome by the wild urge to run for cover. A quick glance back over my right shoulder toward the tree stand confirmed that I'd have to make my stand then and there. The bull was coming on too fast, and a run for the tree would only have alerted him to my spur-of-the-moment ambush. The wind was blowing from the south and if he stayed on course he'd pass by my left side which, fortunately, was also south. I stayed frozen in my tracks until he dropped out of sight in the shallow creek bottom. This gave me a chance to move back to the little spruce tree and ease out of my pack.

I couldn't get down on one knee without getting wet, so I dragged the pack into position and planted my knee on it. Then I raised the rifle, bracing against the tree, to see how it was going to feel. It was okay, so I cocked the hammer and placed a cap on the nipple.

All the while, the bull was marching and grunting his way up the gentle slope toward me. I was beginning to have serious misgivings about leaving the .338 at home. I didn't have long to worry about it, however, as he stopped abruptly just over a hundred yards away at the edge of the meadow. Down went his nose as he sniffed the ground. He slowly lifted his head and looked all around as I crouched behind my pathetic little tree. Then he reached out to the right and sniffed cautiously at a twisted willow. Suddenly, in one fluid motion, he pulled his nose back and turned on his hind legs like a big horse. He was silent as he tried to sneak, undetected, back across the valley to the timber.

I stared in disbelief as he drifted away. It was only then that I realized what had spooked him. I had brushed against the willow on entering the meadow, and he had picked up my scent.

As he strode out of sight into the creek bottom, I hurried across the meadow, pack in one hand and rifle in the other, and made my way among the few scattered willows toward him. I ran out of cover by the time he started up the far slope five hundred yards away.

In desperation, I tried a cow call … nothing. I tried it again, only louder. Still he marched on. I had nothing to lose but my vocal chords, so

I took a deep breath, cupped my hands around my mouth and blasted him with my very best Viagra-enhanced cow call.

It worked. He wheeled around and stood broadside, staring back at me. I quickly belted him with another one while I still had his attention. That ripped it. Now he wasn't "looking" for a cow — he'd found one and he was coming on the dead run. If he were wearing clothing, I'm sure it would all be off by now. As he crossed the creek again, I seized the opportunity to run like hell back up toward the meadow and find a hiding spot in a clump of willows. I had very little choice but to make the best of the situation.

What if the rifle misfired? What if it did fire and, God forbid, he took offence? I didn't have much time to worry about it, with the grunting sounds getting louder and the tops of his antlers and his back looming into view above the willows. He was moving at a fast trot and would likely cross my original path a hundred yards farther south. Perfect. As he charged by across the next meadow I slipped back into my pack, grabbed the rifle, removed the cap from the nipple and headed for the tree stand.

He was headed east, so I was going to have to hurry if I wanted to call him back to the tree.

By the time I reached the north end of the meadow and started up the bunch grass covered slope, I was winded. The bull was by then four hundred yards away and still moving. I watched him until he finally stopped near the timber then gave a sharp cow call toward the east. He immediately turned left and moved northbound along the edge of the timber. At that point, he was probably walking on the same trail the grizzly had traveled earlier. When he moved out of sight behind a small patch of balsam, I crossed a deep brush-choked depression and climbed the last steep pitch up to the tree. A quick glance toward the bull showed him standing still and looking very dejected. Quietly, I eased out of my pack, hung my day pack around my neck along with my bino's, grabbed the .58 and climbed up into the tree.

It was a perfect spot. I had a big branch to sit on, one to stand on and another to rest the rifle across. Jim had this old pine set up perfectly, right down to a place to hang my bino's and day pack.

The bull, meanwhile, was waiting for his newfound sweetheart to get over her shyness. He took out his frustration on a hapless patch of arctic birch, ripping it up with his antlers and throwing it over his back, grunting with every breath.

The ground was dry up above the swampy meadows with patches of arctic birch on the higher ground and bunch grass on the slopes and lower areas. I wanted the bull to come up on top of the ridge to the east of my tree where I could use the rest branch. I watched until he was making noise, then I cupped my hands around my mouth and blasted a cow call down into the arctic birch.

He threw his head up, glaring straight at me. Then, just for good measure, he ripped one more bush out of the ground and came on the run. He was covering ground fast as I placed a cap on the nipple. At two hundred yards he stopped to destroy a little more real estate, so I yelped another call into the brush below. That was it; he couldn't stand it anymore. There was a cow in love over there somewhere, and he was the man for the job.

At a hundred yards, he disappeared into a dry grassy draw. I gave him one more call just to drive him wild, and it worked. At sixty yards he suddenly squirted into view with both front feet flailing the air. Apparently, this is standard procedure in moose foreplay. Having completed this display, he calmly walked toward my left side, still closing the range.

At thirty yards he stopped, perfectly broadside. As I lined up on his lungs, a fleeting thought crossed my mind. This rifle had been loaded since last night. I had forgotten to seal the nipple. I wondered if there was moisture in the flash hole.

It was too late now as I started to squeeze — Snap! Horror of horrors. After all this — a misfire.

The bull jumped straight sideways and stood staring in my direction, but somehow didn't spot me. When he looked away, I pulled the hammer back, flipped the burned cap off the nipple and placed a new cap on. This time I expected it to fire but just in case of a "hang fire," I'd keep the sights firmly on him.

He first began to walk straight away then turned broadside again, walking to my left now at forty yards. This time, pivoting on the rest branch, I lined up on his lungs and squeezed off the shot. Snap! Fizz. Kablam!

The bull spun straight away taking two big jumps, then turned to the right and took three of four big lunges, and disappeared in the tall arctic birch. I could make out the top of one antler, but he was not moving and there was no sound.

With my bino's I searched for any sign of Jim and Duane to the south. At two miles it was hard to tell if they were in the tree stand, and I couldn't see the boat anywhere. The wind was blowing from them to me, so that the sound of the shot was directed away as well. They may not have heard it at all.

Fig 38:
"A sixty-inch bull taken with "Rolling Thunder", my .58 Hawkin."

I carefully climbed out of the tree, reloaded the rifle, got into my pack and headed over to find my bull. First, I went to where he was when I shot, in order to take in the whole series of events. There was a little clipping of hair where he took the first jump. At the end of the second jump, where he turned back to the right, there was a little spray of blood. His deep splayed tracks and the torn up moss showed the tremendous effort he'd put into these last few lunges. From about fifty feet away I could make him out through the thick tangle of arctic birch. After watching him for a minute or two, and detecting no sound or movement, I moved cautiously toward him.

No matter how many moose a person takes in his lifetime, he will always be astonished at the size of a mature northern bull. This one was very likely only four or five years old and was in excellent condition. His perfectly symmetrical sixty-inch-wide antlers would not be legal in Area Seven, since there were only two points on each brow palm.

That familiar storm of mixed feelings hung over me as I walked all around him. I felt sadness at taking his life and thought about the many adventures and close calls he had likely survived with wolves, grizzlies and starvation. On the other hand, a large burden was removed from my shoulders, and my freezer would be full once more. In northern communities a big wood pile and a freezer full of meat are all important.

The daunting task ahead of me was not going away, so I took a deep breath to muster my courage and got with the program. First, I needed a few good photos. In order to accomplish that, I had to clear out a large patch of arctic birch, which I piled in a criss-cross pattern off to the side. I would pile the meat there to cool.

With a clear shooting lane for photos, I set up the camera and tripod. I leaned the old Hawkin against the antlers, pushed the timer button on the camera, and jumped in behind the bull.

At the flash of the camera, the fun ended and the work began. But first there was one last little detail. About ten feet from the bull stood a thicket of arctic birch about seven feet high. I pulled every branch up from six feet around and broke them all off at the height of four feet. Then I gathered them all together and spread my heavy wool jacket over the broken off stubs. This formed a rough table with every branch pulling in a different direction. Then I placed the Hawkin on it, cocked the hammer back, and put a fresh cap on the nipple. If the big grizzly showed up at least I could threaten him with it.

The bull had landed pretty much on his face with his hind legs pointing straight out behind him, so with a little pushing I managed to get him over on his right side. I tied both left legs back to the bases of a couple of arctic birch bushes. Next, I skinned his entire left side and what I could reach of his right side. With the hide out of the way, I removed the front shoulder and placed it on the pile of criss-crossed arctic birch. Then with my knife, I worked my way carefully around the pelvic bone and ball joint and removed the hind quarter. (No easy task for an arthritic old cripple with a sore back) Finally, I took my long-bladed Old Timer and boned out the backstrap from his neck to his hip bone. That was the easy part of the hard part. If I had not been alone, I would have rolled him over and done the same thing on the other side, but for now I had to come up with another plan.

With my little pocket knife and two fingers I started at the pelvic bone and worked my way around the bottom toward the ribs then up past the brisket, opening up the entire gut cavity. He hadn't been eating much, so this chore went quite well.

With the innards out of the way, I boned out the two fillets and laid them out to cool. Then, I carefully removed the heart, liver, and kidneys from the innards and sat back for a well-deserved rest. My back was hurting so badly by this time that I didn't care much if the grizzly came back on not.

I had a bite to eat and a drink of water and got back to work. By the time I got the other hind quarter off, my back was shot. I placed the liver, heart and kidneys in a meat bag and put them in my pack. Then, I took both fillets and put them in as well.

With my coat and pack on and the .58 cradled in my arm, I headed for camp. From the end of the lake, I could see Jim's boat pulled up in front of the meat pole. That was good news. All the meat would be in camp before dark.

Although the trail through the stunted willows near shore was soggy and rough, I felt safer using it, rather than the one up in the timber. As I approached the meat pole and started up the slope to camp, Jim came out of the cook tent.

"Did you see anything?" I asked quietly.

"No," he said, "we didn't see anything. Did you see anything?"

"Yup," I said "I saw a big bull moose."

"Couldn't you get a shot at him?"

"Well ya, I did get a shot at him. Didn't you hear it?"

"No," he said with a puzzled look on his face. "We sat there all day and called a few times but didn't hear a thing. Did you get him?"

"Yup," I said "That I did."

He said, "Really, you shot a moose with that old musket?" I just grinned and nodded my head. He instantly flew into action, as if he had just won a lottery, laughing and slapping me on the shoulder. Dwayne, hearing the commotion, came out of the cook tent as Jim was really getting wound up. "Fergie got a moose with that old smoke pole!" he exclaimed then turned to me and asked "How big is he?"

"Oh," I said " I don't know, close to sixty inches, I guess." That really ripped it.

"Let's go!" he said as he ran around looking for his pack. "Let's go get him."

"Hold it a minute," I said, "I've got to have a bite to eat first." We took the meat out of my pack and placed it on a crude table covered with a few sticks to let the air under it, then covered it with a meat bag. I made myself a sandwich and told them the whole story. Jim still couldn't believe it and was laughing and wiggling as if he had worms.

We grabbed an axe and all our packs and threw them in the boat. I rested my back as Jim rowed us down the lake and Spike followed along the shore. We scouted out a better trail on the way back to the bull — one that would keep us on dry ground most of the way.

I had been away from the kill for a couple of hours, so we approached it carefully, Jim and Dwayne with their rifles ready. Everything was okay, so we went to work cutting the rest of it up. I found the round ball under the skin on his right shoulder. Within three hours, we had all the meat in the boat and were headed for camp. An hour after that, it was all hanging on the meat pole.

That night, Jim cooked us up a big meal of moose fillet, potatoes and, of course, beans. It didn't matter what happened now; the pressure was off and we had meat for the freezer.

After dinner while Jim cleaned up, Dwayne and I played a little crib. He said, "You know, Fergie, I've always dreamed of shooting a moose out in the open buck brush."

I said, "Well if we get a chance, I'll call one up for you. Maybe tomorrow."

That night the fresh moose meat and beans worked its magic. It would have been toasty warm in that tent even if it were forty below zero. I'm sure Spike's eyes were watering.

During the night there was a minor weather change. We didn't get snow or rain but woke up to heavy fog. We couldn't go anywhere so Jim cooked us up a breakfast of bacon, eggs, moose fillet and … beans. After breakfast, we were all standing around in front of the cook tent waiting for the fog to lift. Jim said, "If this doesn't clear up we're going to be stuck here all day."

I took another sip of my coffee and said, "Well I guess we'll just have to call one right into camp then."

He looked at me and asked, "Do you think we can?"

"Why not." I said. "What have we got to lose?"

"What the hell, try it," he said. I put my coffee cup down, cleared my throat and blasted my very best, 'somebody done me wrong' cow call down the lake toward the south. I took another sip of coffee and let fly with another one. Before my call had drifted away, I heard it — "Rupp, Rupp."

I looked back at Jim and he had a wild look on his face. Dwayne was standing dead still staring wide eyed into the fog. "Grab your rifle, Dwayne," I said "We've got to move toward him or we'll end up with a gut pile in the middle of camp!" Jim took his rifle and went up to the trail above camp. Dwayne and I moved quietly along the lakeshore.

Two hundred yards from camp Dwayne whispered, "Fergie, there he is crossing the narrows!" I looked up and, sure enough, he was moving fast. The fog had opened up enough to give us a glimpse of the bull, then, just as fast it, closed in again. We kept moving until we came to the edge of a small meadow at the shore of the lake. Thirty feet from the waters edge, we took our stand behind a stunted spruce sapling. Dwayne checked the .35 Whelen one more time and we were ready for action.

Fig 39:
"Dwayne met his bull out in the open buck brush."

Forty yards up the gentle slope to our left, Jim had taken a stand right on the "Grizzly" trail near the timber. The bull was, by then, within a hundred yards, grunting and raking a patch of twelve-foot-high willows with his antlers. As we listened excitedly to the violent commotion, I noticed Dwayne's leg begin to shake uncontrollably. You could have knocked his eyes off with a stick.

Suddenly, everything went quiet and I seized the opportunity to cause a little more excitement. Turning around, I got down on my knees, cupped my mouth with both hands and with my face right down in the moss gave him another cow call. Instantly, he launched into another tirade of grunts, snorts and destruction. I looked over at Jim and he was coming unglued. Dwayne looked like he was having cardiac arrest! Spike didn't know whether to vomit or wind his watch.

As we huddled behind our little tree, trying to get a look at the bull, another sound got our attention from across the narrows. It was another bull adding his voice to the neighbourhood disturbance. Just then the fog lifted enough for us to get a look at him — we were not disappointed. There, at the edge of the timber, stood an absolute giant of a bull. His heavy wide antlers, standing up like two sheets of plywood, were easily over sixty inches across.

Suddenly, we were snapped back to the task at hand by loud snorting and wildly waving willow tops. With the other bull threatening to steal his girlfriend, I suppose he thought it wise to get this little love affair underway. At the first glance of his antler tips, Dwayne tensed up and raised his rifle. His leg had quit trembling and he was strangely calm as the bull marched right out and stood glaring at us from forty yards. He wasn't sure what we were, but we sure as hell didn't look like a steaming hot cow moose in a mini skirt. He was spinning to the right to bolt into the timber when Dwayne let the shot go. Things happened real fast then. The bull went down with a loud crash as the bullet hit the bottom side of his backbone, directly over his lungs. He was lying there, with his nose pointed straight up, snorting and blowing steam twenty feet in the air when Jim ran into the thick stuff and popped him in the neck.

As the sound of Jim's shot drifted away, a deathly silence closed in on us. Dwayne and I watched the bull across the narrows turn and trot quietly into the timber.

That was that; the fun was over. After a lot of excited laughing and back slapping, we walked back to camp and got the boat, chainsaw and meat cutting gear. Jim cut us out a place to work and I set up the camera for photos. This time there were three of us, so the job was easy. When it came time to bone out the backstraps, I borrowed Jim's hand made bone handled hunting knife. I was shocked. Never before had a knife felt so good in my hand, and I told him so. He said "You teach Dwayne to call moose like that and I'll make you one."

"It's a deal," I said, as we worked away at the moose.

In a few short hours, we had the bull cut up, packed to the boat, floated to camp and hung on the meat pole ... three happy hunters. We would all eat well over the winter and Dwayne's dream came true. He met his bull face to face in the "buck brush."

We took a few more photos in camp and Jim cooked us up some more fillet and 'you-know-what.' We played crib and told lies a little later than usual that night, so late, in fact, that Dwayne and I got hungry again and made Jim cook us up another pan full of fillet.

That night as Jim and I were climbing into our sleeping bags, Dwayne, who was already in his, started laughing. "Fergie, look at Spike!"

"Where the Hell is he?" I asked.

"Right here," he laughed, shining his flashlight at the top edge of his sleeping bag. I looked ... then looked again and spotted just the tip of his tail sticking out of the bag below Dwayne's chin. We all howled with laughter as Dwayne tried to drag him back out onto his own bed.

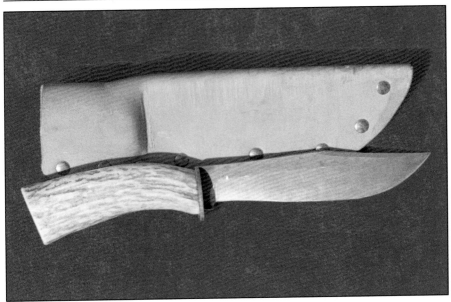

Fig 40:
"A genuine 'Jim Marx Built' bone handled hunting knife and sheath."

This turned out to be one of the best hunts I have ever been on. Hunting partners like Jim and Dwayne don't come along every day, and I consider myself very fortunate to have spent this special time with them. The next spring, Ida and I sold our home in Stewart and, after twenty three years, moved to Clearwater, B.C. The morning we pulled out, Jim came over to the house to say good bye. We were standing beside the moving van talking when Jim said "Damn it, Pat, I wish you didn't have to go."

I said, "Well Jim, we're just going to have to take the time and go on another hunt sometime."

He looked me in the eye and said, "We'll do that." Then he reached behind his back and pulled something out of the waistline of his jeans. "Here," he said, " made you something." It was a genuine 'Jim Marx Built' bone handled hunting knife and sheath. We were both too choked up to say any more. He spun around, walked to his truck and drove away.

•••

About the Author

Born in Kamloops, B.C. in 1948, Patrick George "Pat" Ferguson was raised on the famous Douglas Lake Ranch where his father, Mike Ferguson, was the Cow Boss. Pat started cowboying at the age of nine, riding from dawn to dusk with the rest of the crew. He was just a touch on the wild side, roping his first bear at the age of twelve and breaking his back in three places at fifteen. By the time he finished High School, all the broken bones were beginning to take a toll.

After school, Pat took a stab at underground mining and soon discovered "big money" down in the dust and smoke. At that point he married Ida Brunet — a move that would change his life dramatically. They moved north to Stewart, B.C. where he worked underground at the Granduc Mine. During this time they put all their efforts into raising three healthy children in a happy home.

While many of their friends took their annual vacations in Hawaii or Mexico, Pat and his family headed for the northern wilds.

Fig 41:
Pat Ferguson

After fifteen years underground, Pat's Doctor spotted trouble in his lungs so he quit mining and went to work out in the fresh air where he remains today. He and Ida now make their home in Clearwater, B.C. where the weather is almost always bearable.

•••